Clients Praise *Belief Re-patterning*®

✳   ✳   ✳

"*I had been challenged with back issues much of my adult life, putting up with the discomfort on a daily basis. I tried chiropractic, physiotherapy, Active Release Techniques, acupuncture, massage, Rolfing, yoga, and Pilates, spending thousands of dollars looking for relief. All of these avenues helped a bit, but relief was short-term. Suze walked me through a Belief Re-patterning exercise for my back that took about five minutes, and I haven't had a problem since. It was amazing. I don't profess this to be the magic pill (nor does she); I only know that she helped me, as well as three of my friends who went to see her. One was able to calm his anger, one was able to pass a securities exam that he had failed several times over a three-year period, and the third was able to get back on a plane comfortably again. To me, this illustrates how Suze can get your thoughts working for you, not against you. Why not have everything possible working in your favor?*"

— Kim Wright

✳   ✳   ✳

"*I just want to express my gratitude. It makes so much sense, and I appreciate the clarity. Suze's work has been an instrumental part of my development and growth. I can honestly say that I am a different and better person because of the work.*"

— Michelle Wong

✳   ✳   ✳

"*Belief Re-patterning is exactly what it says it is: a direct and effective route to identifying what blocks you in your life, and it supports you in 'actioning' what strengthens you.*"

— Allison Gillespie, RN

✳   ✳   ✳

*　*　*

*"I was on a wellness journey when I encountered Belief Re-patterning. . . .
Just knowing that we are able to re-pattern our previous life experiences
was my wake-up call. So many doors have opened for me now that
I don't carry that baggage around with me."*

— Donna Law

*　*　*

*"Since beginning Belief Re-patterning, I am more at peace and
centered in myself than I ever have been. When issues arise that
normally would have sent me down the 'tornado of doom,' I just don't
go there anymore. It's now much easier to get to the core of the problem
and work through it. Knowing that I don't have to spend hours or days
trying to figure out why I believe what I do, only that I need to know that
I can change that belief, makes this process more inviting and less
daunting than anything else I have ever used."*

— Michele Benitez

*　*　*

*"There are times in life when you know that what you need is to change
your internal monologue. I felt stuck. The feeling was subtle. I would progress on many fronts; still, I couldn't land the contracts I wanted and was
unable to get to the 'sign on the dotted line' part of the deal. This is when
a good friend suggested that I go see Suze. She was brilliant in her ability
to identify my feelings and help me construct a positive approach to the
issues at hand. As it turned out, Belief Re-patterning helped me with more
than that. Days after our session, an unexpected family crisis unfolded.
Fortunately for all involved, I was peaceful and centered, and managed a
difficult situation with grace and compassion. I have since gone back, and
plan to do so whenever I need to switch to the positive channel."*

— Annette Hester

Belief
Re-patterning®

For J.B.
Enjoy the journey!
Namaste,
Suzy Gazy

Also by Suze Casey

* * *

Audio CD

Conscious Choices, Realized Dreams:
An Introduction to Belief Re-patterning

Booklets

PathWays to Patterns:
A Guide for Belief Re-patterning

Pocket Full of Possibilities:
999 Words to Up Your Vibration

Book

HealthKeeper:
The One Place for Everything Regarding your Health

Please visit:

Hay House USA: **www.hayhouse.com**®
Hay House Australia: **www.hayhouse.com.au**
Hay House UK: **www.hayhouse.co.uk**
Hay House South Africa: **www.hayhouse.co.za**
Hay House India: **www.hayhouse.co.in**

Belief
Re-patterning®

The Amazing Technique for "Flipping the Switch" to Positive Thoughts

SUZE CASEY

INSIGHTS

HAY HOUSE, INC.
Carlsbad, California • New York City
London • Sydney • Johannesburg
Vancouver • Hong Kong • New Delhi

Library of Congress Control Number: 2012930217

Tradepaper ISBN: 978-1-4019-3556-6
Digital ISBN: 978-1-4019-3557-3

15 14 13 12   4 3 2 1
1st edition, April 2012

Printed in the United States of America

＊　＊　＊

To my parents, George and Marion Gould:
You taught me to be true to myself and gave me the perfect
balance of wings and roots.

To Dale:
You helped me find the key to bring me back to me.
You are a touchstone.

To Kathleen:
Your belief in me and in the power of this work is
constant. You are a guiding light.

Namaste

＊　＊　＊

Contents

Preface

✳ ✳ ✳

"I Wish I Had an Off Switch": My Belief Re-patterning Story

Twenty-plus years ago, in a moment of frustrated resignation at the prospect of yet another sleepless night, I yearned aloud: "I wish I could turn off my mind and get the incessant chatter to stop!" I was struggling. I had been on long-term disability and was unable to resume my teaching career because I wasn't getting better. I wanted an off switch. My mind raced as the clock slowly ticked away the hours.

Everyone has inner conversations, more commonly called *thoughts.* When we are healthy and happy, those inner conversations are supportive, and a peaceful silence prevails. When we are unhealthy or stressed—whether physically, emotionally, mentally, or spiritually—calming the ongoing negative inner sound track seems impossible. I had read and studied enough about the mind-body connection and the importance of positive thinking to know that this negative inner dialogue was getting in my way: *Why don't you . . . ? What you should do is . . . ! You'll never . . . !* and *You can't, you can't, you can't.* I needed sleep to regain my health. My mind was working overtime, and the mean and judgmental barrage wouldn't stop. I felt that there was no way out; that's why I wanted an off switch.

My then husband's response to my plea was, "You don't really want to shut your mind off. How will you remember to turn it back on?"

I recognized his logic but replied in frustration, "If I could turn it off, I would never want to turn it back on."

He gently countered, "Yes, you would. Your mind is pretty useful!" His calm, caring voice gave me a new perspective.

But the next morning, the negative thoughts were stronger than ever. I looked in the mirror and wondered, *What is the point?* I had a decision to make. I had been a high achiever, full of energy and upbeat. Now I was housebound and spending most of my time exhausted in bed. I was at a crossroads: get well and truly live, or stay sick and merely exist. I was physically and emotionally spent—at the bottom of a pit.

There are moments in life when you know you are turning a corner, taking a decisive step in a new direction: the *switch* second. This was one of those pivotal moments. I looked deep into my eyes in the mirror and recognized that I had been living out of fear. I needed a more positive perspective. I decided to step over the line. I shifted my focus from my own reflection to that of the window behind me. Outside, the leafless branches of our backyard tree were clearly silhouetted against a bright blue winter sky. As I turned to look outside, a declaration formed deep within me, erupting into the empty silence: "Get me well, and I'll teach others to get well. I am a really good teacher!" This was a new voice emerging: a voice of strength, compassion, and clear intention, a voice that completely silenced the negative chatter.

What was surfacing was my truth, and I made a monumental decision: to live and to live well. I wanted to contribute the best of me to the world. I turned back to the mirror and witnessed the "spark" in my eyes. I looked different! My perspective had changed. My thoughts had shifted. I had flipped the switch—on my own! I decided life had to be easier, and the craziness had to stop—not only for me in *my* life, but also for anyone who was willing to let go of the struggle and experience all of the goodness of life. I decided to *get* well and *be* well, physically, mentally, emotionally, and spiritually.

The supportive voice that emerged from deep within me was a lifeline. In that moment, I became the observer instead of the victim. I moved from fear to the desire to live well. I realized that I, a teacher, now had the most challenging student of my entire career: me! To learn, students need to believe that they are *able* to learn. I needed to believe that *I* could learn to be well. I had to stop seeing myself as sick and broken, and begin to see my potential for wellness. In my declaration I had enlisted the support of my higher power to co-create wellness with me, and the creative thoughts began to flow.

Being both teacher and student required standing back and observing what was going on in my mind. I grouped together the supportive thoughts and called them my *Inner Coach*, and I named the unsupportive thoughts my *Inner Critic.* My mind stopped racing when I began sorting my thoughts as originating from either the compassionate Inner Coach or the harsh Inner Critic. I realized that my Inner Coach spoke to me as my partner had done the night before. It was the same way that I in turn spoke to my partner, my students, and my children. With all of the personal- and professional-development courses that I had attended and taught, with all of the books I'd read, meditation I'd practiced, and journals I'd filled, it had never occurred to me to consciously speak to *myself* that way.

I knew I needed to shift my thoughts, but nothing I had read or studied had really taught me how to do it all the time in a way that worked for me. I understood the concept of positive thinking, but implementing it when I was in the depths of despair or the throes of frustration felt impossible. Everything I had tried worked—sort of. I was trying to *walk the talk,* and I got it intellectually, but a lot of the time, I felt like a fraud. You see, when I was tired, hungry, or emotionally stressed, I would forget all the enlightened stuff I knew, and all the doubts, fears, and anger would surface, causing the Inner Critic to take center stage in my life. I had been immobilized by the stories I was telling myself. I hadn't consciously created my current reality. I knew what I needed to do; I just found it difficult to put it into action. It took bottoming out that morning for me to *get it* and integrate what I knew into my way of being.

I needed to stop thinking that there was something wrong with me. I simply held certain beliefs that triggered habitual behavior and thought patterns. It was time to figure out how to consciously make the switch that had happened while I was looking in the mirror. I needed to encourage myself the way I encouraged those I cared about.

※   ※   ※

For whatever reason, until that day I stared into the mirror, I felt that I was not quite good enough. When I was a child and teenager, I did well yet missed the awards by a fraction of a percent. I was a competitive swimmer with stacks of second- and third-place finishes. Second-string on the volleyball team and not tall enough to try out for basketball, I turned to the arts. I loved being on-stage because I could be someone else, but true to form, I landed the part of understudy to the lead character, or supporting roles.

Looking back from my current, solid vantage point, I can see the patterns that were created by those beliefs, but at the time I was caught up in reinforcing life experiences that came from feeling not quite good enough. My inner conversations reflected my beliefs. I was hard on myself, and had a habit of putting myself down, often with humor, but inside I was hurting. Subconsciously I was making decisions and creating patterns from the feeling that I had to prove myself. Some of the decisions led to great accomplishments as I strove to do just one more thing that would make me feel better about myself. But as a way of life, it didn't work. I would just push myself through to the next project or goal, always from the place of *not quite good enough*. On the surface my résumé was one to be proud of, but my heart and soul were shriveling up. I made some self-destructive decisions and created huge drama in my life. I was unknowingly addicted to the drama of the ups and downs.

Beliefs are neither positive nor negative; they just are. A *belief* is a thought that is repeated so frequently and with sufficient emotion attached to it that you accept it as reality. Even a belief that seems to be detrimental, like the *just not good enough* one that I was carrying, can reap positive benefits. This was the belief that spurred me on. At the age of 21, I graduated with a bachelor's degree in education and began a full-time position teaching junior high school. Over the next five years, in the evenings and summers, I earned a master's degree in education, specializing in the learning process. In my spare time I was a committed volunteer. My life was the perfect reflection of my belief that I had to *do* in order to *be* worthy. During that time I made great social connections that continue to enrich my life. I entered my second marriage and became the happy stepmom to three fabulous young children. I was a part-time professor at the University of Calgary, teaching postgraduate courses, and became an educational consultant for one of the largest school boards in Canada. I was successful, busy, and joyful. Life was very good!

And then things changed. A month before my 30th birthday, in November 1987, I was diagnosed with stage 4 malignant melanoma. My world turned upside down. The prognosis was not good, and I was told to put my affairs in order. My response? I wrote a list of all the things I intended to do in my life, read everything I could find in the medical library on the condition, had the surgery, recovered, and threw myself back into my work at top speed. I would beat cancer! With that achievement I would finally be "enough"!

My strategy failed. In May 1989, I received a second cancer diagnosis. While I was still recovering from the surgery, my husband and I left on a monthlong backpacking trip through Europe, arriving home in time for me to plunge into my volunteer capacity as hospitality coordinator for the local three-day folk festival. Looking back, I shake my head in wonder. What was I doing? All the signs were there that something significant needed to change in my life, but as a type A personality who thought she had to *do* in order to be worthy, I pushed myself back into work with even more determination.

A year later, my shaky foundation crumbled. My body could no longer support what I was demanding of it. One Friday afternoon I came home from teaching feeling a bit under the weather, crawled into bed, and stayed there for three weeks. Then I decided I couldn't be sick any longer, and dragged myself back to work. It was June. My students needed me. I was indispensable. I had report cards to generate. By midmorning I collapsed.

The next six months were a blur of visits to doctors' offices and lab tests. Finally my doctor gave me an ultimatum: take an additional six months to truly heal, or find another doctor. She was frustrated by my single-minded insistence that I could push myself to do whatever I needed to do. Although I'd managed to beat the cancer, I'd pushed myself right into chronic fatigue and fibromyalgia.

Something had to give. I was sick and tired of being sick and tired. Whatever *it* was, *it* needed to change. It took a couple of months of frustration and anger, and feeling like a victim, before that pivotal day in front of the mirror came. That morning I realized I had unknowingly created my then-current reality, and if that was the case, I could consciously create something else, something better. Shifting my thoughts from that reality to what I really wanted seemed elusive. There was a big chasm between the perspectives of my Inner Critic and my Inner Coach. I wondered how could I get my mind working in a positive direction and encourage supportive thoughts?

✳   ✳   ✳

Within a couple of weeks, Louise Hay's *You Can Heal Your Life* came into my hands. The book was comforting and made total sense. Strangely enough, Louise's work also provided the very challenge that was a catalyst in the development of the Belief Re-patterning technique. I loved Louise's affirmations and wanted to agree with them, but sometimes when I repeated them, I felt that I was lying to myself. My Inner Critic would argue with me. Saying the affirmations often created an inner tug-of-war that I couldn't seem to resolve, no matter how hard I tried. I didn't want to give in to my Inner Critic, who was simply backing up those negative perceptions and turning them into my truth by bringing my previous decisions to my consciousness. My Inner Coach had a different perspective, but wasn't adept at gathering evidence to support it.

I puzzled over this until one day, a month or so later, I was a passenger in a car on a busy freeway. I watched the vehicles moving in and through traffic, and it came to me: Trying to switch my thinking using affirmations was like trying to move from the center lane across six lanes of freeway traffic to an off-ramp at full speed. When I tried to cross all the lanes at once, sometimes it worked. I would emerge on the other side out of breath and a little rattled, but safe on the off-ramp. However, more often than not, when I tried to move from a deeply held unsupportive belief to a loving belief by using affirmations in the traditional way, I felt run over by a semi-truck full of all the reasons why I needed to stay where I was. So I remained stuck, immobilized, ending up wherever the highway of fear took me—and definitely not where I wanted to go.

Staying stuck in fear doesn't allow the mind to open up to the possibility of an exit ramp. No exit ramp means staying on the same road, stuck and spinning your wheels. The alternative is to move over lane by lane. The Belief Re-patterning technique is a lane-by-lane approach to affirmations.

Other ways I knew of switching my thoughts were like traveling in the slow lane, trying to wear down the old beliefs. I made a conscious decision to work with the way the mind naturally learns rather than try to force it to work in a different way. No more tug-of-war! No more getting stuck in traffic, being sideswiped, or missing my exit ramp! I developed ways to navigate my thoughts as an experienced driver maneuvers through traffic: easily, purposefully, successfully!

I taught myself, and my body rapidly regained its vitality through that spring and summer. I returned to teaching in the fall of 1991, and began consciously using the exercises and activities with my students. Their learning accelerated!

For a number of years I enthusiastically engaged in refining these learning concepts in my classroom. In my personal life, I enjoyed a balanced perspective without all the dramatic ups and downs that had previously exhausted me. I had achieved my goal of getting well and living well. I navigated a divorce and the changes that brought. I traveled, explored, and did many of the things I had longed to do when I had been ill. Life was good—until another pivotal moment in the spring of 1999. I felt a longing deep inside. Spiritually I was out of alignment, even though, on the surface, everything seemed terrific. The words of my Inner Coach came directly from my core. I grabbed a piece of blank paper and listened. My hand moved across the paper and wrote: "It's time. Teach others to live well."

The very next day, the school board announced a cost-cutting measure: a one-time buyout program for teachers who had been with the board for 20 years or more and who held a master's degree. I qualified. I was excited and terrified at the same time. My entire perception shifted. All day I felt as if I were watching myself from a distance. What was going on with me? I couldn't believe I was actually considering leaving my secure, tenured position that included medical benefits and long-term disability insurance. The final bell of the day rang, and I hopped in my car and drove to my parents' home. I could trust them to help me come to my senses.

They listened as I related the school board's offer. After a moment of silence, my dad said, "Follow your heart." My body relaxed. My heart began to sing. I drove home feeling profoundly peaceful. Sitting on the back deck that spring evening, I found myself looking at the same tree I'd stared at eight years earlier. No longer stark against the wintry sky, it was now bursting with bright leaves shimmering in the sunset. I called my three stepchildren, Camille, Charis, and Dave. Even though their father and I had chosen separate paths, they are my family, and I needed to talk to them. Each of them echoed my dad's words. Darkness descended, and I watched the stars come out. As I went inside to bed, I looked up at the star-filled sky and stated out loud, "I'm looking for a sign." I placed the papers for the buyout package beside the fax machine to be sent in the morning. I needed to sleep on this.

The next morning I woke up laughing! I had dreamed that while walking through a crowd, I felt strongly pulled in a definite direction. I was looking all around, trying to figure out where I was so determinedly headed. And then I saw *The Sign*. It was large, white, and suspended from the ceiling, with an enormous arrow and some words I couldn't make out. In my dream I ran toward the sign, and its words came into focus: GOING PLACES. I laughed from the deepest part of my being—and woke myself up! I got out of bed, walked directly to the fax machine, and hit the *send* button.

An off switch wasn't really what I needed. Instead my mind had *flipped the switch!*

* * *

With any story, there are many starting points, and the journey that led to the creation of Belief Re-patterning was a series of experiences and resulting awareness that came together over time. That summer I attended a Bob Proctor Round Table event. Bob is a well-respected, internationally recognized motivational speaker. I felt honored to be in the audience. Bob encouraged us to be "vigilant" with our thoughts "at all times." It was a great idea, and as I wrote it down, I began to wonder how I could get the same positive results in an easier and more loving way; being *vigilant* felt hard and punishing. I had become frustrated with suggestions that I just change my thinking. That was the exact part that challenged me, and it seemed to me that books and workshop leaders just glossed over it. I knew it was important to keep my thoughts positive, but how could I do that without feeling like a fake? How could I be vigilant *at all times,* when my subconscious was in the driver's seat many more hours than I was able to be aware of my thoughts? Why did it have to take so long?

Bob's thought-provoking comment triggered a deep investigation. Could I develop a way to train my subconscious mind to keep my thoughts positive? Was it possible to reset my autopilot settings and sustain those positive settings so that the Law of Attraction would always manifest in the direction of what I truly wanted? What if I consciously developed powerful neural pathways that would support my subconscious mind to switch my thoughts? After I started experimenting and sharing, refining and realizing, and compiling and creating, I began writing down and tracking my discoveries.

I did not need to be vigilant at all times. I discovered that I could proactively train my subconscious mind to do it for me, and it was happening quickly and easily.

* * *

I decided to pull together what I had learned into something that anyone could do, regardless of age, education, experience level, or situation. That decision was the conscious beginning of Belief Re-patterning and the systematic start of the synthesis of years of experience, study, practice, and thought. I translated my own experiences with changing my self-talk and combined that with what I had discovered in my classroom. For a number of years I explored the technique with willing friends. They were excited by their results and started telling others. The phone calls starting coming, and I began seeing several clients a week.

I taught my mind to provide new perspectives quickly. I became less reactive and more responsive to situations and challenges in my own life. I combined what I was coming to understand through energy work with what I knew about education and how our minds learn. I stopped seeing myself as broken and in need of healing, and began recognizing that I had learned some patterns that no longer served me. If I had learned a pattern that wasn't working, I could learn a new one that *would,* and I didn't have to know what the old pattern was or where it began. My current way of being did not need to be my future.

I officially opened my full-time private practice in the fall of 2001, offering sessions to individuals and families. Soon I was seeing up to 30 clients a week using the techniques and activities I personally had used to regain my own health. In 2002 I coined the term *Belief Re-patterning* to describe the specific technique of using patterned statements to shift your thoughts, and in 2003, at the urging of my clients, I began teaching Belief Re-patterning courses. The first practitioners graduated in 2004. The Belief Re-patterning technique continues to spread, largely by word of mouth.

* * *

Reviewing my life from a more secure place, I can now see many of the patterns clearly. I practice re-patterning my own beliefs daily and enjoy a life beyond what I used to dream of. I live in a purposeful and fulfilling way, and like who I am, how I'm changing, and who I am becoming. I am at peace with myself and where I've been, and excited about where I am going! And, I'm keeping the promise I made that wintry day: I'm teaching others how to get well and be well.

As you experience the inevitable changes of life, your beliefs need to change. Belief Re-patterning works whether you recognize the patterns or not. It works whether you know where it all started or are completely baffled by how you got to this place, and it works whether you need to talk things through or are tired of retelling your story. Whatever situation you find yourself in, you know you are ready to leave the struggle behind. Similar to where I was 20 years ago, you may have arrived at the deep knowing that change needs to happen, and wish there were an easy and effective way to go about it. Or you may already be conscious of the patterns and their roots, and are looking for an efficient method of moving beyond those old beliefs that bind your growth and hamper your ability to manifest what you desire. You may just be stuck and want relief. Wherever you are in your journey, I'm glad we've connected. Belief Re-patterning will support you in making real, lasting change and positive growth a reality in your life.

I'm thrilled to bring this way of being to a wider audience through my connection with Hay House. This book relates my lived experience, and I found it challenging to determine a starting point. Thankfully, my editor, Alex, brought to the work an observational perspective that helped me navigate. I'm deeply grateful for her insight and dedication in supporting me to create this book, which effectively presents a wonderful way for you to learn the technique and experience the profound benefits of Belief Re-patterning.

Pivotal moments and turning points provide clarity and direction in this journey called life. This book speaks to that journey. You'll discover how to navigate your thought processes to achieve your personal goals, dreams, and desires. You'll learn to calm your inner conversations and develop daily practices of reinforcing your Inner Coach. You'll step out of the unsupportive patterns of your Inner Critic, not by examining the old patterns or going over the details of the past, but rather by creating new, supportive patterns. This will happen with more ease and speed than you can imagine! Actively engaging in the activities and reflections will personalize your experience. At **www.suzecasey.com/blog** you can ask your questions, share your *Aha*'s, and gain additional support. I look forward to hearing from you!

Whether you want to expand your current reality with more ease and joy, or are healing from physical or emotional challenges, Belief Re-patterning works. When each of us contributes the best energy we can to our world, we help raise the energy of the planet as a whole. It takes very little light to dispel darkness. Lighten yourself, and you lighten the world. It truly is something we each can contribute. Let's journey together.

Namaste,

Suze

Calgary, Alberta

❋ ❋ ❋ ❋ ❋

Introduction

✳   ✳   ✳

What Is Belief Re-patterning?

You understand the importance of positive thinking, but implementing it when times are tough takes a lot of discipline. What if you could train your mind to shift to positive thoughts automatically?

Solidly based in cognitive learning theory and educational psychology, Belief Re-patterning works like a *reset switch* to direct your thought process. You will learn how to consciously switch your thoughts from what hasn't been working, and open up to new possibilities. You'll also learn how to create the clarity of mind that allows for a more spiritual way of being in the world through consistent, positive inner dialogue.

I have always been fascinated with how our minds work, and during my 20-year teaching career, I developed ways of supporting all kinds and ages of learners. You didn't come with an owner's manual for your mind. You learned but you probably didn't learn *how* you learned. This technique makes conscious the subconscious learning process we all use every day. Belief Re-patterning works with the way your body, mind, and soul already learn. The process feels natural and easy, because you are actually wired to live this way. Bringing this subconscious ability to your conscious awareness will allow you to make your thoughts work *for* you. And practicing this powerful technique will integrate the learning into your subconscious, allowing you to use it for the rest of your life.

Belief Re-patterning opens the door to inspiring yourself from within. You are a being of energy, and your thoughts, emotions, and actions all transform that energy into the reality of your experiences. Imagine a way to tap into the best of you and create from an authentic place of alignment—body, mind, and soul. While you are *learning* about the Belief Re-patterning technique, you will also be *re-patterning* your own beliefs. You'll gain a great deal by simply reading *Belief Re-patterning;* however, your ability to re-pattern will be considerably enhanced by the experiential learning offered through the activities in these pages. Personalizing your learning with examples from your own life will integrate the re-patterning process into your subconscious.

This book relates some of the pivotal moments and learning that I experienced while developing the technique, reflections from my clients, and real stories of how Belief Re-patterning has impacted their lives. It also provides you with hands-on activities and practical exercises for igniting your inner motivation, realizing your potential, and contributing your best to the world. Are you ready to step over the line into self-acceptance and appreciation of your uniqueness?

Can You Actually Re-pattern Your Own Thoughts?

Many of my clients first come to get help through a challenging period or situation. They are amazed by how rapidly they move to a solid place from which they can take real action. They also discover the benefit of regular check-ins and, rather than wait until they are in crisis, build on the strengths of their previous sessions. My vision was to develop a method that everyone could proactively learn to do, so I began teaching Belief Re-patterning as a technique for personal growth.

I am grateful to all who have entrusted their journeys to me. Through observing their learning, I came to truly understand the power of living in this amazing way. I've worked in person or over the phone with thousands of individuals in one-on-one Belief Re-patterning sessions. I take on the role of the Inner Coach, helping them identify the emotions that hold old patterns in place and then leading them through a series of individualized Re-patterning Statements. Depending on the person and the particular circumstances, we usually complete between two and six re-patterning series during a first session. Clients then have activities that reinforce the re-patterning, many of which are included in this book. Most of my clients commit to ongoing Belief Re-patterning sessions to enhance their own daily practices. These sessions may be as frequent as biweekly for someone in a state of rapid change or challenged health. Occasional check-ins are often all that's needed for those who are comfortable with their re-patterning skills.

Clients, students, and practitioners have been asking me to publish the illustrative stories and anecdotes I use in individual consultations, workplace seminars, and the courses I offer, and provide a handy reference filled with activities they can use to support themselves in their own Belief Re-patterning. This book is my answer to their requests, and it's completely accessible to those who are totally new to these concepts as well.

Having been used and tested extensively, the technique holds true for people of all ages, crossing gender, economic, and educational groups. It works to solve challenges and realize dreams. What everyone has in common is the desire for something different, and a readiness to embrace real and lasting change.

Do any of these characteristics apply to you?

- Have you done personal-development work but aren't getting the results you desire?

- Have you wondered if there's a way to change how your life just always seems to go?

- Are you confident that there's a way that will work for you, and are you open to finding it?

- Are you a lifelong learner who is tired of being told about your "potential"—by yourself or others?

- Are you actively living your life and wishing for the serenity of *being*, but getting caught in the busyness of *doing?*

- Have you ever held yourself back or sabotaged yourself when you came close to a goal?

- Do you know you want to make a change and have some of the ingredients, but need support in pulling it all together and making it work?

- Do you want strategies for changing the way things have been, and support in creating what you *want* instead?

BELIEF RE-PATTERNING WORKS . . .

- . . . with people who are falling apart, as well as those who really have it together but know they can sharpen their skill sets. We have all found ourselves in both places!

- . . . when you are in crisis or calm.

- . . . when those around you are experiencing challenges—for both them and you.

- . . . in the workplace and at home.

- . . . whether you think it will or not.

You've been told about the Law of Attraction and encouraged to develop a sunny perspective, so you understand the importance of positive thoughts. You agree, and on your good days, this all works beautifully. But what about the times when you slip? How about when you are overtired or hungry, or just not yourself? There's more to positive self-talk than simply happy talk, and you know that it doesn't work to pretend you are upbeat when you are not. You understand the concept that what you put out comes back, yet you find yourself feeling frustrated, angry, or depressed. The next thing you know, you are beating yourself up for thinking negative thoughts and sending that out into the world. You know you don't want to create more negative thoughts. You know it isn't healthy and isn't bringing you what you desire. You begin berating yourself for being out of alignment with what you know to be true to you, and there you are, sliding down the slippery slope of an unsupportive pattern.

I understood how damaging negative thoughts are and wondered if there was a way I could get my mind to move automatically to the positive, a way I could train my mind to function supportively. My teaching background and academic pursuits helped me understand how we learn. When I made a conscious decision to stop wondering what was wrong with me and asking why I "can't," "haven't," or "didn't," or investigating why this had to happen to me—when I *crossed the line* from focusing on the deficits and applied what I knew about learning—the crazy-making questions stopped. It was when I explored how to take that conscious decision and transform it into a subconscious habit that the development of Belief Re-patterning began. If *you* have ever wondered, *How do I get to the other side of the line?* then this book is for you.

Whether you are just beginning or are a practiced veteran of personal development, *Belief Re-patterning* helps you open the door and walk through with practical and beneficial ways to integrate your learning. In the chapters to follow, you will learn to observe both your Inner Critic and your Inner Coach. You'll strengthen your Inner Coach and learn to move through the judgment your Inner Critic expresses. Through this process you'll feel and observe your progress, and your true self will emerge. You'll experience results in all areas of your life.

This book provides you with a how-to tool kit for creating positive inner dialogue. You'll learn how your mind works, with reinforcing practices that you can integrate into your daily activities, and you'll discover the ease with which you can train your mind to *flip the switch* to positive thoughts.

> "If you don't change your beliefs, your life will
> be like this forever. Is that good news?"
> — ATTRIBUTED TO W. SOMERSET MAUGHAM

What Makes This Book Different?

There are thousands of courses, seminars, books, tapes, and programs that emphasize the importance of positive thinking. After studying and teaching personal development for years, I was frustrated by my inability to really integrate what I knew to be true. The authors, presenters, and teachers encouraged me to think positively, but didn't give any concrete ways to make that happen. I was motivated, but my motivation would wane. I'd start and then stop. I understood but often seemed to fail at integrating the learning, especially in times of stress, and then I would beat up on myself and create a whole new series of challenges. I wanted real and lasting positive change, and I wanted it quickly and easily.

The suggestion to *switch your thoughts* generally doesn't work well. Attempting a simple switch from put-down to positive adds fuel to the fire of the Inner Critic. The Inner Critic's comments increase and intensify, and an internal tug-of-war is on between the old pattern and the new idea. Belief Re-patterning works because the focus is on switching the emotion you are feeling rather than trying to change the thought. Since strong emotion and repetition are the ingredients that turn a random thought into a learned belief, it made sense to me to focus on switching the emotion.

Using Belief Re-patterning, you'll learn to consciously disconnect the unpleasant (⇓) emotion from any challenge, and move to the way you would rather feel: the opposite, pleasing (⇑) emotion. Throughout this book, I'll use (⇓) to indicate thoughts and beliefs that pull your energy down, and emotions that you would like to experience less frequently. The (⇑) indicates thoughts and beliefs that support you or raise your energy, and emotions you'd like to experience more.

At many points I will ask you to *feel into* your body and mind's responses to statements or activities. By this, I mean you will want to be present to physical sensations you're experiencing and tune in to the messages you receive from all of your senses. When I ask you to feel into something, notice whether your energy moves (⇑) or (⇓). Is your body's response to the statements pleasant, unpleasant, or neutral? Listen to the thoughts that come forward. Both your Inner Critic and Inner Coach will give you feedback. Is it supportive and something you would say to someone you were trying to help (⇑)? Or are the comments sarcastic or judgmental (⇓)?

Your observation of what's happening in the present with your thoughts and accompanying emotions means that you shift your focus away from how things have been. You don't need to identify the pattern, just how you are feeling and how you *want* to feel. Identifying these emotions allows you to create a new reality—one that allows your dreams and desires to manifest. Practicing the Re-patterning Statements throughout the book teaches your mind a way to habitually switch your emotions, by providing a supportive structure for new thought patterns, which in turn result in positive changes in your belief system. A more positive belief system creates changed actions and reactions; in other words, your behavior switches, allowing for different results. This conscious connecting of your body's emotional language to your mind's receptivity to learn something new allows you to make real, profound, and lasting positive change in all areas of your life, not just the current situation.

We are all wired to learn and grow, and approaching your personal and professional development from a place of *learning something new,* rather than *fixing something wrong,* raises your personal vibration. Your inner conversations become far more supportive, and you find the peace of mind you've been seeking. From that lighter place, your Inner Coach calls the plays, and your body, mind, and spirit work together. The Inner Critic stops being a destructive force and supports the Inner Coach by pointing out the contrast and bringing previous awareness and learning to your consciousness. Your Inner Critic and Inner Coach work together to provide uplifting and supportive inner conversations, leaving the old internal tug-of-war behind. You are developing and shaping your belief system to support you in creating positive change.

We all lead full and active lives. Most of us have great intentions to make a change but don't. Change requires focus and practice, and if you are like me, after a few days the best-laid plans sometimes fall by the wayside. I'm sure this has happened to you: You get new information, understand the value of the exercises or practices, and know it would make a difference, but you are just too busy to get to it today, so you put it off until tomorrow or next week. Tomorrow never comes. What we need to set new learning into place is a quick, conscious activity that we can practice to the point where it becomes a habit. That's how we all learn, and that's what Belief Re-patterning provides.

And So We Begin!

You've made the decision to change, and you are ready for something different. You are prepared to create more positive thoughts and change the way you speak to yourself. Today, stop pushing the river. Let go of wondering where, why, and how you've been pushing against whatever you've been struggling with. Today, gently enter the current by bringing to mind the times you have been in the flow and riding the wave. Focus your thoughts and questions in that direction—consciously.

Through Belief Re-patterning you'll learn how to create balance and encourage constructive self-talk. Equally important, you'll discover guaranteed ways of quickly and almost effortlessly getting back on track when life's stressors have pulled you off. You'll engage your Inner Coach and begin experiencing your life with a new, supportive approach. The skills you'll master will positively impact your life in ways you cannot imagine. Once upon a time, you learned basic mathematics, and continue to apply that learning daily. You learned to read, and that skill supports you in all areas of your life. Belief Re-patterning is like that.

Human experience is a journey. At times we encounter rough roads, other times clear pathways; sometimes we seem to be on a superhighway with nothing stopping us, until we turn a corner and find ourselves mired in the muck. All of us have traveled each of these ways at various times in our lives. Whether you are on a slow, meandering stroll or a fast-track sprint of discovery, Belief Re-patterning is a supportive companion for your journey. Appreciate your decision to move forward, to grow, and to learn. From this moment on, you can choose to create your life in a more conscious way, using all your experience and knowledge, and you can train your subconscious mind to *flip your switch to positive thoughts* automatically!

* * * * *

An Orientation to This Book

In this book you'll experience some of the structured statements I've used over the past decade to teach individuals and groups to re-pattern their own beliefs, and find many exercises and activities you can use to create positive thoughts as a normal way of being. Jump into the process and share your experiences, ask questions, and get clarification on my blog at **www.suzecasey .com**. On this website, you'll also find a free, downloadable companion journal that follows the book's format and provides more specific examples and details for the exercises, activities, and Re-patterning Statements to support you in learning this material. As you read the book and practice the activities in your journal, you will not only learn about the technique, but also actually re-pattern some of your unsupportive beliefs!

As a classroom teacher, university instructor, and course facilitator, I follow the energy of the group and use *teachable moments* to create learning opportunities for each participant. Because I don't have your immediate feedback while you are reading, I anticipated what you would need and when. Everyone learns differently. Some like to receive the structure of the material first, followed by examples to reinforce their learning. Other learners find that storytelling supports their learning best, because the structure emerges through anecdotes.

A common denominator is the power of experience. Regardless of your preferred learning style, to really grasp something in a deep and meaningful way, you need to experience it. You could read this entire book in one day, and if you do, I encourage you to then go back and work through the exercises and activities in each chapter over time. If you've previously encountered some of the concepts and activities in this book, I urge you to explore them again from the perspective of Belief Re-patterning. Each chapter includes anecdotes and illustrative stories, along with a discussion of strategies and concepts for personal development. Sprinkled throughout the chapters are experiential learning opportunities called *Re-patterning Statements, Try this On! Practices,* and *Quick Reflections.*

Re-patterning Statements: The Basis of the Technique

In each chapter you'll find sample Re-patterning Statements. Saying them out loud as you come to them creates the structure that your subconscious mind will quickly begin using to flip the switch. The purpose of the statements is to shift your mind's perceptions. As you progress through the book, you'll experience Belief Re-patterning while training your subconscious to use the *lane-by-lane* structure of the technique. It may feel repetitive because that's one of the ways in which we learn. I've used common themes to illustrate the material, so whether or not the exact content of the Re-patterning Statements resonates with you, reading them out loud is an effective and efficient way of learning. Feel free to change the specifics to fit your personal situation, but keep the structure intact.

It's also important to breathe in deeply through your nose after you say each statement. Then exhale through your mouth. As you do so, allow space for your mind's response to the statement. This combination of breathing, reading the statements aloud, and listening for any internal response keeps your mind present to the process and helps you integrate the learning. Through this experiential learning, you will train your mind to not only re-pattern your habitual thoughts, but also process new information in a more supportive manner. The Re-patterning Statements throughout the book will all be formatted in the same way as the following example:

RE-PATTERNING STATEMENTS: BASIC EXAMPLES

I forgive myself for believing that the way things have been is the way they need to stay.

I don't like that feeling, so I give myself permission to let it go and explore a new way of being.

I can either believe that things will always be the same, or I can explore a new way. I can't do both at the same time, so I consciously choose to explore a new way of being.

I am free to experience my life in a new way.

I like the feeling of experiencing life in a new way.

I am open to experiencing life in a new way.

You'll discover the details about each of the six types of Re-patterning Statements and how they work in Part II, "Flipping the Switch." In Part III, "Positive Thoughts as Your Way of Being," you'll learn how to make the re-patterning more effective by integrating the technique into your daily activities.

Try This On! Practices

Another way in which we learn is by developing consistent habits. It's easier to develop a new habit by tying it to an already existing activity or habit. The suggested practices are practical and can be readily incorporated into an already-full lifestyle. Implement the suggestions gradually, beginning with the ones that resonate with you the most. The quick practices throughout the book will reinforce your Inner Coach and support you in uncovering methods of using your Inner Critic in a positive and growth-directed way.

Quick Reflections

Learning is reinforced through reflection, and reflection is most effective when you write your responses. I invite you to respond in your journal to the exercises and questions as they occur throughout the book. Doing so will personalize the information and provide real opportunities for you to integrate your learning. The three to five minutes you invest in these Quick Reflections will provide context for upcoming content in the book, and help you become more observant of the patterns in your language and actions. There is a distinct and tangible energetic power to the written word.

You may find that it works better for you to read the book from cover to cover, and then come back to the beginning to work through the chapters and do the written reflections. However you incorporate the Quick Reflections, you'll discover what works best for your learning style and lifestyle.

Both the Quick Reflections and the Try This On! Practices appear as shaded exercises, formatted as in the following example. I encourage you to download your complimentary journal right away and try this introductory reflection before you delve into Part I.

Quick Reflection:
INTRO

Reflect for three to five minutes on the following questions to clarify your intention for interacting with this book, and visualize where you would like it to take you. This provides a snapshot of where you are as you open yourself to the process of Belief Re-patterning. Setting your intention before beginning anything is a powerful learning strategy that we'll explore more thoroughly. Close your eyes after reading each question and listen to the inner conversation:

- What do you believe to be true about yourself?

- Which of those beliefs would you most like to re-pattern?

- What specific changes would you like to create in your life through Belief Re-patterning?

You will want to refer to your responses throughout your reading, so jot them down in your journal. Knowing where you started will give you a reference point for the changes you'll experience as you re-pattern your beliefs.

Part 1

*   *   *

CONNECTING BELIEFS AND LEARNING:

What Is Possible?

Chapter One

FEAR IS REAL:
Use It to Create Something Better

* * *

*"Too many of us are not living our dreams
because we are living our fears."*

— LES BROWN

Fear, or some form of it, is the only thing that has ever held you back or limited you. It's uncomfortable and fairly common, and can be huge and debilitating. Fear is very real. Fear is powerful! It needs to be. Its main purpose is to keep us alive. Acknowledging that power right up front begins the process of change. When you are experiencing fear, you are out of your comfort zone. To learn and grow, you must leave that comfort zone.

Naturally, everyone feels unpleasant emotions. Those uncomfortable feelings are normal. They let you know you are off track or someone has pushed your boundaries. The purpose of Belief Re-patterning is not to eliminate uncomfortable emotions. You will continue to get angry, experience frustration, and feel scared. Belief Re-patterning makes a difference by helping you choose to move through those feelings in moments, minutes, or hours instead of remaining stuck in them for days, weeks, or decades. You've got an incredible tool that, when applied consciously, allows you to use the feeling you don't want (⇓) to shift to a feeling you do want (⇑) quickly and effortlessly. You'll recognize and respond to your emotions rather than react or have them take over. Belief Re-patterning actually connects the unpleasant emotion to a preferred one so that the next time it shows up, your mind has a built-in off-ramp. You are literally teaching your mind new habits and a different way to process information and experiences. What you practice consciously moves into the realm of the subconscious and becomes a new way of being, acting, and believing.

There are four basic ways you can experience any emotion:

1. Ignore it.

2. Hang out in it.

3. Feed it.

4. Use it.

Every emotion, from love to fear, is experienced in one of these ways. For a long time I tried ignoring fear, pretending it didn't exist, putting it behind a big wall, and hiding it with false self-confidence. The wall eventually tumbled down and nearly took me with it. For years I hung out in fear by wondering why it was happening to me, and turning it over and examining it. I would look to include others to hang out in fear with me by talking to friends and family in attempts to justify the way I felt. Trying to figure out the root cause of the issue, or where it came from, feeds fear. Letting my mind run undisciplined through lists of other things that were wrong simply focused my attention on the fear and created more of it. The fourth choice—*using the fear*—is where we'll begin your personal Belief Re-patterning journey.

The Origin of Fear

> *"Fear is a darkroom where negatives develop."*
> — ATTRIBUTED TO USMAN B. ASIF

Fear is real in the moment, and our bodies respond by producing chemicals that course through our veins and place us in fight-or-flight mode, which translates into our daily lives as arguments, procrastination, and avoidance. In fight-or-flight mode, the chemical concoctions our bodies produce block our conscious, reasoning, and creative minds and allow our subconscious intelligence to take over. This is how we are hardwired to survive, and it's an extremely useful physiological response to real and imminent danger. We don't have time to think, just to react.

But real and imminent danger is not what you face on a daily basis. Usually it's simply the expanded space of something new or different from normal that puts your body on alert. It might even be something that your conscious mind finds exciting but your subconscious experiences trepidation around, perhaps causing a small voice inside to call, *Watch out!* Your subconscious mind controls your behavior and causes you to react rather than respond. The subconscious is full of stored memories, all the result of previous learning. Some of those memories support your growth; others simply get in the way of new learning. Consciously you know you are in no danger, but you feel fear or some of its close cousins, like worry and anxiety, because that is what your subconscious has stored.

It just doesn't make any sense. You know that you are capable, that you can do this, that everything is all right, but you still have that uncomfortable gnawing deep in your belly. Like me, you've probably spent a lot of time and energy, and maybe even money, trying to figure out where the fear, anxiety, depression, or anger came from. One day I recognized that trying to figure out the source of these (⇊) feelings fed them and created more of the same. Fear has held me back and stolen many of my creative and exciting ideas. In the past, it has derailed fabulous plans, kept me from deep and meaningful relationships, and stood in the way of my bringing my best self forward. Fear contributed to a plethora of habits that kept me from moving forward with ease and grace. That has all changed. Fear no longer defines me, and it doesn't need to define you.

Using Fear in a Purposeful Way

All of our emotions are purposeful, including fear. Using fear to propel us through our real and imagined challenges is extremely useful. But we overuse fear, and we use it in the wrong way. The movie industry has turned this emotion into entertainment, and we devour it. In our day-to-day experiences, we go to fear so readily and hang out there too long. We examine it, turn it over and over and over again in our minds, allowing it to control our thoughts and actions.

Extreme fear can completely immobilize us. I met Anne when she was in her late teens. An intelligent and beautiful young woman, she had always been shy, but after she had completed high school, the fear of interacting with others had isolated her. She had challenges with leaving the house. For over a year, she had only gone out when she absolutely had to and always with someone. A trusted family friend of Anne's brought her to my office.

Anne's tear-filled eyes were downcast, and her arms remained crossed even when I extended my hand to greet her. As she and her friend settled into the comfy chairs in my office, I explained the Belief Re-patterning process to her. I would use muscle testing (a technique I discuss in Chapter 5) to identify an emotion that was dragging her energy down. Rather than explore that emotion, I would guide her to identify the positive opposite and then use those two opposing emotions to create a specific, individualized series of Re-patterning Statements to help her shift her energy. Anne was relieved that we didn't go into dissecting where the fears had come from or how long they had held her hostage. We began re-patterning, using Re-patterning Statements similar to the ones you'll encounter throughout this book. As we progressed through the process, I made the statements more specific to Anne's situation based on the feedback she received from her thoughts and memories.

Within 15 minutes Anne looked into my eyes. Her tears had subsided, she was breathing more deeply, and her shoulders were relaxed. By the end of the hour, we had re-patterned five related emotions that were hold-ing old beliefs in place. Anne smiled and eagerly booked a second appointment to continue the process. Beliefs gather in layers, and this technique gently removes the old layers while creating a foundation of new, support-ive beliefs. Anne's friend was amazed by the transforma-tion that she witnessed in Anne.

A week later, the two returned, and Anne greeted me with a hug. Although she had encountered some tough times, she had also experienced some significant breakthroughs. She had gone for a walk every day on her own, and was now comfortable driving alone. With her friend beside her for reassurance and support, Anne and I continued gently re-patterning her limiting beliefs. I was thrilled when she arrived on her own for her third appointment. This was visible evidence that her confi-dence and courage were increasing.

On her fourth visit, Anne excitedly told me that she had just come from the university, where she had regis-tered for the fall semester. Over the next few years, while she completed her undergraduate degree, she studied Be-lief Re-patterning to develop her own abilities, and the time between appointments continued to expand. Anne joined the drama team, began dating, and treated herself to a trip to Europe on graduation. Through re-patterning she created the life she had always desired. Twelve years later, Anne is a successful businesswoman who travels internationally. I enjoy hearing of her adventures when she calls in for her annual tune-up!

❋   ❋   ❋

Some of my clients say, "I just want to get rid of the fear—forever." That's like saying, "I have a sore elbow, so let's amputate my arm." In the moment, when the pain is intense, you may truly believe that amputation is the best plan. However, as your arm heals, which is the natural thing for our bodies to do, you are very, very glad to have your arm intact.

The same sentiment occurs with any uncomfortable emotion: fear, anxiety, worry, anger, jealousy, or sadness. When these feelings are intense, we will do almost anything to make them go away, preferably forever. But once we've graduated from a few schools of hard knocks, we recognize that those very trying times are what have led to some of our great accomplishments and realizations. Strangely, they enrich our lives. Losing these emotions isn't the answer; using them to create something better is. Just as it is natural for our physical bodies to heal with good nutrition, our emotional and spiritual selves also heal and become stronger when we create supportive thoughts.

Most of us struggle against challenging times and difficult emotions, believing that struggle is a necessary part of the process. That is true of the butterfly, whose struggle to escape the cocoon builds the necessary wing strength to carry it for thousands of miles. Trying to free the butterfly by helping it on its way will actually damage it so that it can't survive. Fortunately our lives are not the same as that of the butterfly. Accomplishment does not need to be hard, and struggle is not necessary for survival. As a young woman, I focused a lot of my time on wondering why my personal struggles, and those of my friends and family, had to be so painful and protracted. I wondered at the struggle I observed in the world around me. I decided it just had to be easier. Life is a *dance,* not a struggle, and I wanted to get on with the dance!

I am not suggesting trying to eliminate uncomfortable emotions. What I am advocating is that we use these emotions purposefully to point ourselves in a supportive direction. We can leverage them to create what we truly desire, and clarify who we genuinely are and what we deeply value. Having an effective way to process our emotions allows us to move forward with increased joy, ease, and gratitude.

The Re-patterning Statements are not simply affirmations. They provide a framework, an actual structure, for your mind to use over and over again. Your subconscious mind is learning the steps and stages, and will begin running the patterns automatically whenever an uncomfortable emotion surfaces. As you become familiar with the technique, you'll find the Re-patterning Statements popping into your mind as you go about your day and even when you are sleeping.

Consciously navigating this structural framework teaches your subconscious mind to cue your conscious mind in ways that effectively help you process the emotions, learn any needed lesson, and reap the benefits of the experience without all the drama and pain. Christie, an elementary schoolteacher, mom, and longtime client, puts it this way: "I feel so grateful to experience Belief Re-patterning, as it has helped me release the limiting subconscious beliefs that were unknowingly running in the background. It is truly a painless process that creates growth and self-fulfillment—positively life changing!"

Imagine no longer being stuck in an unsupportive belief pattern or recurring thought process. Your Inner Coach will easily shift your fearful emotional state by asking, *How long do I want to experience this?* With Belief Re-patterning you have the tools to shorten the time frame to moments, and use that fear to create something better.

You Can Re-pattern Fear

Have you thought about this?

- Every moment you spend in anger is a moment lost forever to love.

- Every minute you've felt frustrated is a minute you didn't feel peace.

- Experiencing fear steals calm.

Let's do some re-patterning around fear—any fear, one that you have right now, had in the past, or anticipate coming across in the future. An interesting thing about learning is that once you learn something and practice it consciously, it then moves into your subconscious, where it is available for you to apply to future situations. The new learning can also be applied to past situations, allowing you to work through old memories with a new perspective. Saying the Re-patterning Statements out loud throughout the book will give your conscious mind the practice it needs to develop this subconscious habit. Sometimes the examples, like the one that follows, will be generalized, meaning that I'll give you most of the words. Even if the specific situation doesn't really apply to you at this time, all of the Re-patterning Statements are based on common themes I've encountered with clients. As you progress through the book, you will find more specific Re-patterning Statements that will allow you the opportunity to individualize them to your unique situation and needs. Instructions and examples to help you personalize your Re-patterning Statements will be bracketed and set in italics.

Remember to breathe deeply (in through your nose and out through your mouth) after you've said each statement. This helps you *feel into* your body's response. Whenever you see a blank in the Re-patterning Statements, verbally fill it in with the first thing that comes to mind. The spaces are there for you to personalize the Re-patterning Statements with examples that are meaningful to you. If you find it easier to write down the statements and fill them in as you go, use your journal.

Let's re-pattern. Sit quietly for a moment and pick one fear to hold in your mind as you say the statements out loud. Give extra emphasis to the boldfaced words.

RE-PATTERNING STATEMENTS: BASIC RE-PATTERNING FOR FEAR

I **forgive** myself for believing that I need to hang on to this fear.

I recognize this fear, and I **forgive** myself for believing that it is my only response.

I've experienced this fear long enough, and I **forgive** myself for believing that I need to stay here.

I give myself **permission** to find the opposite of the fear, which is calm.

I give myself **permission** to walk through the fear; it's not helping.

I give myself **permission** to learn whatever this experience is here to teach me and let the fear go.

I **choose** to let the fear go; it does not define me.

In the places in my body, mind, and spirit that have held that fear, I **choose** to let it go and experience calm.

I consciously **choose** to release that fear and experience calm.

I am **free** to focus on what being calm feels like, right now.

I am **free** to bring calm into my body, mind, and spirit.

I am **free** to do something right now that creates calm for me.

I love being calm. It **happens when** I _____ (⇑).
[Fill in the blank with a specific example; here are some ideas: watch a sunset, hold my sweetie, walk in nature *. . .]*

I **know what it feels** like to be calm. I was calm yesterday when I _____. *[Fill in the blank with a recent experience of feeling calm.]*

I **like being around** calm people like _____. *[Fill in the name of a person you know who is frequently calm.]*

I **am** increasing the calm in my life today.

I **am** becoming calm.

I begin to **define** myself as calm: it feels like *me*.

Reading aloud focuses your attention and supports you in remaining present. The vibration of the words as you say and hear them reinforces the meaning in a deeper way than does reading them silently. While you were reading the statements out loud, you may have noticed some physical changes. Your breathing may have become deeper and easier, and your heart rate likely slowed. The more you develop your ability to *feel into* your body's responses, the easier it will be for you to become observant and then make supportive choices.

You also likely noticed that there were more statements than in the example you encountered in the "Orientation to This Book." There are six distinct stages to the Belief Re-patterning technique, each with a particular wording, in boldface, associated with it. You'll learn more about this and the purpose of each of the six stages in Part II, "Flipping the Switch." For now, it's important to notice that the number of statements will vary depending on your inner dialogue. In this series I used three of each stage to illustrate some ways to build the statements. As you move through the Re-patterning Statements in each chapter, you'll begin to feel when you need to create additional statements for yourself.

The Re-patterning Statements guide your mind to think in a certain way. You may have been aware of some thoughts surfacing as you read them, and we'll cover how to use those thoughts to build supportive inner conversations in Part II. The power of these structured conversations to create new thought patterns is easy to attain, and through experiencing the statements, you will integrate the technique for shifting your emotions. Moving fear to calm changes your perception and allows the conscious mind to, once again, be creative and productive.

While you were saying the Re-patterning Statements, did your Inner Coach agree with the supportive thoughts? That's the goal, and soon it will begin to happen, if it hasn't already. Did your Inner Critic respond by arguing using doubt or sarcasm? Pushing that critical voice aside only causes it to pop up later, so ignoring it isn't the answer. Hanging out in or feeding the fear is what you want to avoid, so use the (⇓) messages from your Inner Critic to point you toward what you want instead. Rather than hang out in the darkroom developing more negatives, use that fear to identify the opposite (⇑) feeling and transform the emotion into what you would rather feel. Hanging out in an (⇑) emotion that is supportive builds your Inner Coach, and strengthening your Inner Coach is far more productive and effective than trying to wrestle with your Inner Critic!

Quick Reflection:

STRENGTHEN YOUR INNER COACH

Let's build up your Inner Coach by focusing on feelings of love: the places, things, and people you cherish. Close your eyes and finish this statement:

Some of the people, places, and things that I love, past and present, are _____.

You may wish to make a list in your journal so you will be able to reference it when you create your individualized Re-patterning Statements.

Here is an example of some of the people, places, and things I love:

• The ocean at sunrise at Port Douglas, Queensland, Australia

- My grandbabies, Casey, Jacob, and Natalie; and my niece, Lyla

- My friends Kathleen, Dale, and Phil

- The orange, gold, and pink sand dunes in Vietnam

- A cup of tea made using mint from my garden

- The feel of the water on my body when I'm swimming in Lake Okanagan

- The sound of the whales from Rebecca's boat in Maui

- The sunset over the mountains I see from my desk

- The full moon illuminating the fresh snow at the mountain cabin near Banff

Notice that I didn't just say "family," "friends," and "sunsets," so make sure to be specific with names and locations in your own list. The more specific your examples are, the stronger and higher the vibration becomes. Close your eyes and say, "I love my friends." Breathe in and notice the feelings in your body. Then choose a couple of friends and fill in their names as you say, "I love my friends _____ and _____," again with your eyes closed. Do you notice the difference in the (⇑) emotion when you use specific examples?

When you are going into a dark place, it's always good to have a flashlight. Focusing on the things you love before looking at the fears provides that flashlight. Learning anything happens more quickly and with greater ease when you begin from a place of strength. Thinking about what you love and care about provides a solid foundation for you to then observe the fears you've worked through successfully in the past. Acknowledging the fears you have overcome further strengthens your Inner Coach. What fears have you encountered and successfully moved through in your life? List them in your journal; they will support your re-patterning.

I made a list of fears that I successfully moved through so that you can see how to build specific statements in the next series of Re-patterning Statements. I have overcome the fear of:

- Living on my own

- Never being loved

- Heights

- Being ridiculed by others for what I think about

- Not regaining my health

- Not being good enough

- Talking to lawyers

- Snakes

Listing what you love and some of the fears you've overcome puts you in a strong place to examine your current fears. I know that I continue to experience fear around:

- Letting down those I care about

- Hurting others

- Bungee jumping, bobsledding, hang gliding, and parasailing

In your journal, jot down three to five of your known fears. Just make a quick list. Acknowledging the fear is one thing; hanging out in it is another. Hanging out in the fear doesn't support you; it just generates more fear. Pretending that the fear doesn't exist by shoving it aside merely strengthens it. Writing down your fear allows your mind to know that you are paying attention. Making a list of the tasks you want to accomplish in a day or a week clears your mind, enabling you to focus on what you are doing, rather than all of the things racing through your mind that you are trying to remember. The same works for fears. Writing them down sends the message to your mind that you will work through these fears—just not all of them *right now*.

Carrie had some very deep fears that she had developed as a child. They were wreaking havoc in her adult life with her relationship, career, and self-confidence. She told me she felt as if she had tried everything, but she *hadn't* tried Belief Re-patterning, so she was open to it. She wanted a change but had been unable to get past the fear. After her initial session, we booked another one for three weeks later and then had a follow-up six weeks after that. I didn't hear from her or see her again for some time, and then one day, a note from Carrie arrived in the mail:

> I am so grateful that I found you and could be a part of Belief Re-patterning. I have manifested greatness in my life, and you were a part of this success. I came to you about a year and a half ago, at the lowest time in my life. I was seeking a solution, a different way of thinking, and a genuine feeling of hope and faith that I would be okay. I am forever grateful. I have applied this different way of challenging my thoughts when I become fearful and doubtful. What you do is life alter-ing in the most profound ways. Thank you for believ-ing in me, coaching me, and helping me to change. Thank you for sharing your secret.

Carrie knew there had to be a way out of the fear and depression she was living with, and she was actively seeking it. Belief Re-patterning has been successful at helping thousands of people work through deep and very real fears, and it will help *you* as well. Remember, you don't need to retell or relive your story to re-pattern the fear; you just need to be open to learning another way of processing your thoughts and emotions.

* * *

For these next two series of Re-patterning Statements, choose one of the unsupportive fears you listed. Set yourself up for success by selecting one that is more of a surface fear than a deep-rooted one. With practice, you will be able to re-pattern any fear you choose, but while you are learning the technique, pick one that is inconvenient rather than life altering. Think about that fear while you read these general Re-patterning Statements. Remember to voice each statement aloud, breathe in deeply through your nose, and exhale through your mouth.

RE-PATTERNING STATEMENTS FOR ALL FEARS

I forgive myself for **believing** that I need to hang on to this old fear.

I give myself **permission** to let go of this old fear; it is in the way of my growth.

I can stay in that fear, or I can grow with ease, and I **choose** to grow with ease.

I'm **free** to grow and change with ease.

I **remember** old fears I've worked through. I grew through those fears, and I can grow through this one.

I **am learning** to grow through fear with ease.

General Re-patterning Statements become more powerful when you personalize them by using real examples. With your chosen fear in mind, do some advance preparation. Copy your answers into your journal. These are not Re-patterning Statements; they are simply guided inner prep work, so you will have the ingredients for personalizing your own Re-patterning Statements. You'll name the specific (⇓) feeling attached to that fear (*don't want*), and identify the opposite (⇑) feeling (*want*). From the list you made of the things you love, choose something you could easily do right now (*action*) to help you create the (⇑) feeling you want. I'll walk you through the process using one of the fears I listed, putting my specific statements in italics for you to use as a guide.

The fear I choose to personalize in this re-patterning process is _____.

The fear I choose to personalize in this re-patterning process is not having enough time to do everything.

When I think about this fear, I feel _____ (⇓) [don't want].

When I think about this fear, I feel rushed.

I would rather feel the opposite of those feelings, which would be _____ (⇑) [want].

I would rather feel the opposite of those feelings, which would be relaxed.

One thing I could do right now to help me feel _____ (⇑) [want] is _____ [action].

One thing I could do right now to help me feel relaxed is pick some mint and make tea.

Once you've completed the prep work, you are ready to create your personalized version of "Re-patterning Statements for All Fears." Remember to say them aloud and breathe after each statement.

RE-PATTERNING STATEMENTS FOR SPECIFIC FEARS

I **forgive** myself for believing that I have to keep feeling _____ (⇓) [don't want].

I forgive myself for believing that I have to keep feeling <u>rushed</u>.

I give myself **permission** to focus on being _____ (⇑) [want].

I give myself permission to focus on being <u>relaxed</u>.

I can feel _____ (⇓) , or I can feel _____ (⇑); I can't feel both ways at the same time. Right now, I consciously **choose** to feel _____ (⇑).

I can feel <u>rushed</u>, or I can feel <u>relaxed</u>; I can't feel both ways at the same time. Right now, I consciously choose to feel <u>relaxed</u>.

I am **free** to focus on being _____ (⇑).

I am free to focus on being <u>relaxed</u>.

I **create** the feeling of being _____ (⇑) right now by _____ [action].

I create the feeling of being <u>relaxed</u> right now by <u>making a cup of mint tea</u>.

I like **being** _____ (⇑). It feels like me.

I like being <u>relaxed</u>. It feels like me.

Do you see how you've used specific examples and changed the statement to keep your mind interested, and receptive to the message? These statements create a link between the emotion you don't want and the one you do. In my example, my mind has linked *rushed* with *relaxed*. The next time I feel *rushed,* my Inner Coach now has *relaxed* available as an option. I used an uncomfortable emotion to create something better, and so did you. Reinforce the re-patterning you've just completed by writing your example in your journal:

My mind has now linked _____ (⇓) with _____ (⇑).

The next time I feel _____ (⇓), my Inner Coach now has _____ (⇑) available as an option.

Through the Re-patterning Statements, I have consciously given an instruction to my subconscious that whenever I feel _____ (⇓), I choose _____ (⇑) instead.

Try This One! Practice:
FOCUS ON WHAT YOU LOVE

Continue to strengthen your Inner Coach by focusing your mind on the (⇑) people, places, and things you experience throughout the day. Most of us take many of these (⇑) experiences for granted. Look for and acknowledge whatever raises your energy, actively building your Inner Coach's ability to find (⇑) examples when you most need them. Tying this practice to something you are already doing will help you remember to land on the upside.

My client Roy had severe digestive challenges. I suggested that he connect eating with the practice of focusing on things he loves. Every time he prepared to eat, he stopped and listed the things he loved that had occurred since his previous meal. Just before breakfast, he thought about reading his son a bedtime story, laughing during the movie the previous night, the warmth of his bed, the good-night hug from his wife, the early-morning sun on the mountains, the invigorating water of his shower, and the pungent smell of his morning coffee. Once he had raised his energy, he began to eat. Roy did this before every meal for a week, and his digestive challenges disappeared.

Years ago, whenever I walked toward my car, I consciously practiced focusing my mind on the (⇑) people, places, and things I had just experienced. Interestingly enough, when I am in a tough space, this habit consciously kicks in and helps me remember what is right in my world.

Pick something you'll be doing several times today, and make a commitment to tie that habit to the practice of focusing on what you love. Help your mind be receptive by coming up with different examples of what you love, and feel your energy rise!

David Roth is a wonderful singer-songwriter (**davidrothmusic.com**) whose unique perspectives on life make his songs an absolute delight. Here's his take on fear:

Forgetting
Everything's
All
Right

What a great perspective on fear: *Forgetting Every-thing's All Right*. Fear is real, and it now provides an op-portunity for me to check in with myself to see if the fear has any merit. Fear that is the result of a bear star-ing at you differs from the fear of not getting everything done. The fear of intimacy that stems from abuse differs from the fear of losing your keys. It's important to know that every fear you hold that doesn't support you can be re-patterned. The sample Re-patterning Statements we walked through will begin the re-patterning process and help you remember that *everything's all right.*

* * *

As with learning any new concepts, practice will strengthen your neural pathways, and we will get to that in the next chapter. At this stage my intention is for you to get the feel for plugging your own information and ideas into the Re-patterning Statements. You always have choices, and you are the one who decides how you will feel at any given time about anything. Re-patterning doesn't take away what happened to create the fear; it *does* allow you to choose a different perspective on it. You've begun the process. You are choosing a new way to speak to yourself, and we'll continue consciously prac-ticing it until the new, supportive way becomes habit.

Learning anything starts with a need or desire for change. Then it's a matter of discovering the incremental steps that lead you from where you currently are to where you want to go. A new habit is formed through practicing those steps. You integrate the new learning when you link it to something you already know. It's helpful to have a model, someone who has *been there, done that* to watch and learn from, and we all learn best when learning is fun and purposeful. Encouragement and celebration are also essential aspects of this process. Belief Re-patterning uses the way you learn to support you in creating what you choose. It's not about removing fear. It's about using fear to create what you want instead.

❋   ❋   ❋   ❋   ❋

Chapter Two

HOW DO WE LEARN?
A Look "Under the Hood"

✳ ✳ ✳

"If a child can't learn the way we teach, maybe we should teach the way they learn."

— ATTRIBUTED TO IGNACIO ESTRADA

It has always fascinated me that no one perceives or deduces information in the same way. When I'm trying to figure out how something works, I observe small children. They learn in incremental steps. For the most part, they find it easy and, generally, fun. We encourage, mentor, and model for them. When little kids experience frustration, they usually back up to the previous comfortable and successful way, and try again. They are like thirsty sponges soaking up new information and new ways of doing or being, and practicing whatever it is until it becomes habit. Adults learn in the same way. We practice something new until it becomes habitual. If there are challenges, we back up and try another approach. However, if others were harsh with us in the past, we may have shut down along the way. We may have learned to put ourselves down and judge ourselves harshly, and that gets in the way of our ability to learn and grow.

In order to learn, the mind must be open and receptive. Experiencing fear, anger, or frustration—and feeling small or stupid—shuts down learning. Teachers, coaches, and parents help students open their minds by reminding them of times when they were successful, of activities that worked, and of challenges that became accomplishments. Once there is a solid place to anchor them, new concepts are introduced, providing an opportunity for expanding awareness and understanding. Learning is about making connections between what we already know and something new.

The quote from Ignacio Estrada that opens this chapter became a guiding focus in my teaching practice. I created and designed learning activities that met learners where they were, and I used them in my classroom and shared them with other teachers in workshops and seminars. One wonderful day, while I was observing a group of students interacting, I came to my single truth about learning:

If individuals believe in themselves and their ability to learn, they learn.

All of my research, observations, and implementation came together in this one realization: if they believe they can, they will. My teaching practice shifted from content and methodology to focusing on helping my students believe in themselves. When they believed in themselves, their learning came naturally, and they excelled.

What Are Beliefs?

All of our actions and behaviors are a reflection of the beliefs we have created in response to events and situations. They are the products of our conditioning, perspective, and filters. We created these beliefs—which are not facts but merely truths *for us*—in order to make sense of our world. Then we began to act as if they were facts.

Most people think that their beliefs just *are* and that changing them is either extremely difficult or impossible. A belief is a thought that is charged with emotion and repeated so often that it becomes a pattern. When your mind has a pattern, it doesn't need to give conscious thought to what it is doing; the subconscious can just run the pattern. Changing that pattern can seem challenging, but it doesn't have to be. You've experienced rapid shifts in your beliefs. Your belief about a person has been completely changed by a conversation. Your belief about the world has been shifted by one phone call or an image on television. The birth of a child or the death of a loved one can instantly alter your beliefs about your world. Strong emotion will re-pattern any belief.

Beliefs are your anchors. They can give balance in stormy weather, allowing you to explore and return to safety. They provide a solid base, a connection, and can be a source of confidence. However, beliefs, like anchors, can also be counterproductive. Try to sail out of the harbor without lifting the anchor! The once-useful mooring becomes dead weight, and progress is severely impeded. The same holds true with your beliefs. Positive beliefs support you. Limiting beliefs drag you down, hold you back, and make progress difficult.

Have you ever seen a full-grown elephant on a tether? Do you know how these mighty animals are trained to stay in one place like that? Baby elephants have a chain placed around an ankle, which is then attached to a steel spike. Try as the young elephant might, he can't stray because the chain keeps pulling him back. Eventually he decides that it's painful to move and he can't go forward. As he grows and becomes stronger, he doesn't realize that he could easily pull out the stake. The pattern is in place. He believes he can't move forward, so he doesn't. At some point a stick and a rope replace the steel spike and chain. The adult elephant remains held in place by his own beliefs about how his world is.

The same thing happened to you. When you were younger, you learned certain patterns about the way life works. You may have become older, wiser, and stronger, but you are so used to looking at the world through the belief system you developed that you don't realize that what was once a chain and spike is now a rope and stick. You can shift many beliefs with relative ease. Every belief you have, whether supportive or unsupportive, whether based on truth or misperception, is held in place by emotion. When you change the emotion, you change the pattern of the belief.

What Are Emotions?

Emotions are the messengers and communicators of the body, and are neither good nor bad. How we *use* them determines whether they support or limit us. They are extremely helpful to us when we learn to listen, but can be detrimental when they are stifled, blocked, or ignored. Physical sensations and feelings in the body are translated by your mind with a thought into an emotion. Recall the palpable excitement on Christmas morning when you were a child, or how you have felt while waiting for a loved one at the airport gate. Now think about the physical sensation of fear. Your body's response to both scenarios is extremely similar: your stomach grips, your heart beats faster, and you may begin to perspire. What is different is the thought you attach to the physical feeling that creates the emotion of either excitement or fear. You feel the physical sensations and think *Oh no!* and the thought translates the physical feeling into fear. If, however, you feel the same physical sensations and think *Oh yes!* you experience excitement. The physical sensations are the same, but depending on what thought is attached, different emotions or states of being are created.

Your body is continually creating chemical compounds in response to your feelings. These chemicals are then sent throughout your body via the bloodstream to the cells. You've experienced this with adrenaline; you can feel it coursing through your body. You've also experienced the shiver of joy that makes your whole body tingle from the tips of your toes to the top of your head. The chemical concoction is different for each emotion, reinforcing the physical response, which then feeds additional thoughts that, in turn, send more reinforcement to the body, triggering it to send out more chemicals in response. Our cells have receptors for the chemicals being sent through the bloodstream. Like little catcher's mitts, the receptors grab onto the chemical mixtures and inform the cells of how they need to respond. The process is self-perpetuating so that when we become fixated on an emotion or a state of being, and the chemical mixture remains consistent, our cells replicate, creating more receptors for the chemicals that our bodies are creating for that frequently experienced emotion.

For example, if you are continually frustrated, your physical body actually creates more cell receptors for the chemical concoction of frustration that floods through your system. Similarly, if you are experiencing peacefulness as your way of being, your cells physically create more receptors for peacefulness. By consciously focusing your thoughts on the emotions you want to experience more, you are actually stimulating your physical body to create more receptors for that emotion.

Quick Reflection:

BELIEFS YOU ARE AWARE OF

One of the wonderful aspects of Belief Re-patterning is that you do not need to know what a belief is in order to re-pattern it. However, by working with some of the ones you *are* aware of, you will understand the relationship between beliefs and emotions. Set a timer for two minutes, and in your journal write down the beliefs that you know you hold. Ask yourself, *What do I believe about money? What do I believe about my relationships? What do I believe about my future? What do I believe about my past?* Using a new line for each belief you write down, list as many as you can in the time allotted. Then read each belief out loud and ask yourself, *What is the feeling attached to this belief?* Write the emotion beside the belief. Then indicate whether you'd like to have more (⇑) of this feeling or less (⇓).

You'll find it helpful to refer to this list as you create your personalized Re-patterning Statements throughout the book.

How Belief Re-patterning Affects Your Receptor Cells

Processing limiting emotions more efficiently and effectively enables you to make clearer decisions about how you want to be. By re-patterning the emotion that holds an unsupportive belief in place, your mind sends a different message to the part of the brain that creates the chemical compounds. The result is that your physical body produces less of the associated compound. When the cells replicate, there are fewer receptors on them for that (⇓) emotion, which then diminishes the cells' need for that specific chemical combination. You will not remove all of the receptors for the (⇓) emotion, but you can significantly reduce the number, which means you will experience that state of being less frequently. Similarly, the process of consciously choosing supportive emotions in a proactive manner also enables you to actually change the way the receptors duplicate on individual cells, creating more receptors for the chemical compounds of the (⇑) emotion.

At the same time that you are affecting the receptor cells through re-patterning, you are also forging a link between the (⇓) emotion and the (⇑) emotion, connecting them in your thought patterns. This provides a proactive option the next time you experience the unsupportive emotion. This link acts like a bridge between the two emotions so that when your conscious mind registers one feeling, the opposite is also registered, allowing you to consciously choose which to experience. Rather than subconsciously reacting to the experience, you have a moment of proactive, conscious choice. The connections or links your mind habitually makes are called *neural pathways*. When a neural pathway is created, learning has occurred. Neural pathways are created through emotion and repetition.

Try This One! Practice:

USE VARIED REPETITION TO YOUR ADVANTAGE

We learn through repetition; however, the repetition needs to include variation for effective learning to take place. Let me illustrate this point by asking you to say the following statement five times, breathing in through your nose and out through your mouth after each time:

I am understanding and kind to myself.

Feel into the response of your body and mind as you breathe. Most people notice that even when the content is supportive, repeating exactly the same thing over and over again creates doubt or frustration.

Imagine your partner, your child, or a dear friend saying to you in a heartfelt way, "I love you." Your energy would rise, and you would smile and feel good. What would happen if, a minute later, that person said exactly the same thing again, in just as meaningful a way? You might wonder what was up, but would likely still respond favorably. By the third time in as many minutes that your loved one repeats, "I love you," you will begin to question whether this person needs to borrow money or your car. Even though the content and delivery of the message are both supportive, repeating it in exactly the same way over and over again creates doubt in the mind of the recipient. If, however, that same individual comes up to you the second time and says, "I love how you are always there for me!" you hear this differently. Adding even more specifics with the third statement, "I can always rely on you, and I love that about you!" deepens the feeling of love that you experience.

Incorporating this concept into the way you speak to yourself, you may have noticed that repeating the supportive statement five times stirs up your Inner Critic. This is why sometimes stating the same thing over and over again doesn't work. If you are creating any (⇓) feelings with the repetition, the positive affirmations just don't sink in. Shifting the language slightly with each repetition and adding specific examples is an effective way to increase the results you get from saying affirmations, and it really works when you are using Re-patterning Statements.

Try this by saying, "I am understanding and kind to myself" out loud in five different ways, breathing in and out after each statement. You can either make up your own statements or use these examples:

I am understanding and kind to myself.

I am understanding and kind to others and myself.

I am learning to be more understanding and kind to myself every day.

Every experience is an opportunity to be understanding and kind to myself.

When I am learning something new, I am understanding and kind to myself.

Feel into the physical sensations. Listen for feedback, and be present to and aware of your personal responses. Was the feedback different this time? Perhaps it was gentler or your Inner Coach came forward with some specific examples.

Using repetition strengthens our neural pathways, and varying each statement slightly keeps the mind receptive to the statements. Just as our physical bodies gain strength through repetition, so does the mind. Most of us who lift weights at the gym do so not because we want to compete professionally in weight lifting, but rather because we know it's a good, proactive thing to do. Physical trainers know that the repetitions become easier when they make it fun, use incremental steps, vary the exercises, and focus on what's working. We go to the gym so that when our bodies are physically stressed, we have the ability to withstand challenges without injury. Simply put, I lift weights so that I can shovel snow or lift my grandchildren with ease.

Strengthening the mind makes sense. Waiting until a crisis point would be like waiting until you break your back to begin lifting weights. Belief Re-patterning is a proactive approach that makes changing your beliefs fun and incremental. There is an ease to life that comes from focusing on what's working and moving forward from there. When you stop focusing on solving problems or figuring out what went wrong, your Inner Critic calms down, and your inner conversations become useful and supportive. Proactively exercising your Inner Coach will support you in times of stress, giving you the ability to navigate life's challenges more effectively and with greater ease.

Your Conscious and Subconscious Minds

Most of us have a general idea of the difference between our conscious and subconscious minds, but knowing some specifics about the attributes of each will clarify why Belief Re-patterning works to train your mind to automatically flip the switch to positive thoughts.

Processing information and making connections, your conscious mind is your *learning center*. It develops understandings and perceptions based on new information or experiences, and then hands off that data to your subconscious. Your subconscious mind has no ability to make decisions. It sorts, stores, and retrieves the data your conscious mind hands it. Your conscious mind learns patterns that your subconscious mind stores and then runs.

The first few times you sat down at a computer keyboard, you used your conscious mind to *find* each of the letters. As you spent more time at the keyboard, you *learned* the pattern of the keys through repetition, and those patterns were stored in your subconscious. The speed with which you could translate your thoughts into words on the screen increased. Most of us can type our names faster than any other word. That is because you've created a strong neural pathway for typing your name through repetition and emotion. Your subconscious mind is an incredible storage system. It holds information and facts you've gathered, as well as your perceptions and beliefs about that information. It sorts and prioritizes the data according to emotional impact, and when triggered sends it back to your conscious mind.

You may drive the same route daily to and from work. Every time you've driven it, you have maneuvered the car easily, arriving safely at your destination. Sometimes you barely remember the drive unless something significant or unusual happens. Your subconscious mind is your own personal *autopilot,* and actually causes your behavior more than 90 percent of the time. If you have ever had the misfortune of being in an accident on that well-traveled route, you noticed that the next time you drove past the accident scene, your body went on alert. Despite the fact that you have successfully driven that road thousands of times, the highly charged emotion of that one event makes that memory a higher priority in your subconscious. Logically, you should remember all of the times you've driven safely on that road, but because you are wired for survival, even a minor accident triggers a strong emotional charge in your subconscious. In an emergency situation, the subconscious mind overrules the conscious one, because it's thousands of times more powerful. This is a useful survival feature but one that can get in the way when you are moving forward in your life, because the subconscious mind works with habit, or *the way things have been* until now.

The set of beliefs and patterns that put your daily world on autopilot are accessed by your subconscious mind at lightning speed. You may not remember creating those patterns. Research shows that many of them were created before your second birthday. Since those patterns were learned, they can be *un*learned through re-patterning.

Your conscious mind processes information slowly and methodically. You've experienced this when you were learning something new and asked whoever was teaching you, "Give me a moment while I wrap my head around this. Okay, now I've got it!" That's the moving of the new information from your slowly processing conscious mind to your rapidly playing subconscious mind. Your conscious mind is creative, making new connections and forming interesting ideas. Your subconscious mind is the realm of habit. It's what keeps you sane. If you had to think about everything you did as you did it, you would tire out. Your subconscious mind is always running in the background. Your conscious mind comes into play when you decide to engage it.

Some of the differences between the abilities and roles of the conscious and subconscious minds are summarized here:

Conscious Mind	Subconscious Mind
Slower	Faster
Logical; decision maker	Autopilot
Creative	Habitual
Thrive	Survive
Gathers and processes information	Sorts and hangs on to information
Decides what to store, process, or forget	Remembers but cannot decide
Rationalizes, compares, contrasts	Does not distinguish between truth and untruth
Builds the story to prove you right	Prioritizes information based on emotion
Is engaged when you choose to use it	Is always running in the background
Runs the show less than 10 percent of the time for most people	Runs the show more than 90 percent of the time for most people
Creates connections between new ideas and known information	Strengthens old knowing through years of support and patterns laid over the belief

Belief Re-patterning uses the cooperative and synergistic process that already exists between your conscious and your subconscious mind. Through the practice of re-patterning, you change the emotional charge. Autopilot programming that is no longer supportive or necessary is, in essence, *rewritten* when you consciously identify the emotion that held the old belief in place, and then re-pattern it with the opposite (⇑) emotion. These rewritten programs are then sent back to the subconscious mind to be stored and run as needed, along with the (⇑) emotional charge that will keep the new pattern a higher priority.

Do You Recognize the Power of Your Reticular Activator?

The *reticular activator*—also known as the *reticular activating system,* or RAS—is the part of your brain where the world outside of you meets your inside thoughts and feelings. The base of the reticular activator is connected to the spinal cord and constantly receives direct input from all of your body's senses. The RAS controls central-nervous-system activity and has dominion over such functions as wakefulness, attentiveness, and sleep. It looks for the fit between the outside environment and what's happening within you. It screens and sorts information, and provides the neural connections needed for processing and learning new information. The RAS focuses your conscious mind on what requires your attention, and blocks out the rest based on the past experiences stored in your subconscious.

You may have had direct experience of your RAS the last time you bought a car. Your internal *screen* adjusted to let in specific information about the make, model, and color of your new car in order to align with the decision you made to purchase that particular vehicle. Did you notice that all of a sudden, you saw a lot of cars that were the same as yours?

Another example of the powerful ability of your RAS is familiar to anyone who has been at a large gathering where many people are conversing. All conversations other than the one you are engaged in are a jumble of voices until your name is spoken from across the room, at which point you hear it loud and clear! Your attention is immediately drawn from the conversation you were consciously engaged in to look for the person who spoke your name. This is your reticular activator at work!

Your reticular activator acts as a filter that determines what your conscious mind notices. It screens all of the information coming in from all of your senses based on your beliefs and experiences, and the task at hand. The RAS is driven by how you are feeling, and is responsible for determining what bits of information you pay attention to and what goes by unnoticed by your conscious mind.

We need this screen to help us deal with the sheer amount of information coming at us constantly. What better way to screen than to only allow in the information that supports what we already believe!

This is absolutely ingenious—unless, of course, the beliefs that are being reinforced are not supportive of your personal growth and development. If beliefs are holding you back, your reticular activator will continue to look for visible evidence of *why you can't* instead of *why you can.*

When you use your conscious mind to decide what emotion you want to experience, you are setting your reticular activator. Rather than requiring you to always remember the specifics, the series of Re-patterning Statements use repetition and emotion to create new neural pathways. This learning becomes another habitual pattern that the subconscious mind stores and has readily available to apply to any future situation.

By training your mind using Belief Re-patterning, you disconnect the unsupportive pattern so that your mind no longer focuses on or pays attention to input related to the old belief. Using Re-patterning Statements ensures that your reticular activator is focusing on positive input. You are working with how you learn, and actively developing changes in your perceptions.

In preparation for the next series of Re-patterning Statements, close your eyes and ask yourself, *How do I feel about re-patterning my beliefs?* You may have mixed feelings, like one of these pairs:

Apprehensive? (⇓)	Excited? (⇑)
Confused? (⇓)	Confident? (⇑)
Uncertain? (⇓)	Ready? (⇑)

Choose a set of emotions that describes how you are feeling. If none of these fit, write in your journal what you are experiencing, and place a (⇓) beside any feelings you would like to experience less often when you learn something new. Then ask yourself, *What is the positive opposite of this feeling?* Write down that word beside the first one, and put a (⇑) next to it, marking it as a feeling you'd like to experience more frequently. If you are experiencing several different emotions, choose a pair of emotional opposites in which one feeling limits and the other supports. Re-patterning involves linking the two emotions to give you the off-ramp we explored earlier.

The two emotions you have identified get plugged into the blanks as you say the next series of Re-patterning Statements out loud. Remember to breathe deeply after each statement and note any feedback from either your Inner Critic or your Inner Coach.

RE-PATTERNING STATEMENTS FOR BELIEFS

I **forgive** myself for believing that I need to hang on to feeling _____ (⇓) about re-patterning my beliefs.

I give myself **permission** to feel _____ (⇑) about re-patterning my beliefs.

I can feel _____ (⇓) or _____ (⇑) about re-patterning my beliefs. I consciously **choose** to feel _____ (⇑).

I am **free** to experience _____ (⇑) whenever I re-pattern.

I **remember** creating a more supportive belief about _____ [give a specific (⇑) example], and thinking about that makes me feel _____ (⇑) about learning to consciously re-pattern.

I **am** _____ (⇑) about the positive effects I make possible in my life through re-patterning.

You may have noticed that you needed to change the form of the word or rearrange the statement a bit for it to make sense. When students are learning this in Belief Re-patterning courses, I encourage them to write the sentences down in their journals. Hearing the statements as you say them, combined with writing them down and seeing the written form, is a powerful learning strategy that you may want to use.

Where Did Those Beliefs Come From?

The beliefs you hold are all learned. You may or may not remember learning them. Some of your beliefs support you, and some limit you. You now have an understanding of how your mind and body reinforce beliefs and keep them in place, but you may still be wondering where those beliefs originated. Why did you create them in the first place? Where did they come from?

Your belief system is created by the decisions you make in response to what happens. It is constantly changing and is built from many sources. Researchers are looking into the possibility that some beliefs are passed to us in our DNA, and prenatal psychology has shown that a baby absorbs a great deal of information before being born. Studies have proved what mothers have known for centuries: the fetus responds to stimuli like sound and light. In addition, your mother's bloodstream was connected to yours, and the chemical concoctions her body made in response to the specific emotions she was experiencing traveled through the placenta and into *your* body, strengthening certain receptor cells. While you were forming physically, you were also forming emotional receptor cells to support you in the environment into which you eventually would be born.

When you were a young child, your belief system was further developed through the conditioning you received from your family, friends, and schooling. With input from the media, society, peers and associates, the books you read, the music you listen to, the films and television shows you watch, and the thoughts you have, your belief system is in a constant state of change. You may not have had any control over what you arrived with or what happened in your childhood, but you have complete control now. Every belief can be re-patterned. Your body continuously responds to the events, situations, and people around you, as well as your thoughts about all of this input. Your beliefs are a collection of perceptions that you can change.

Imagine taking all the energy you've expended in trying to figure out where all the old unsupportive beliefs, feelings, and ideas came from, and applying that energy to creating a supportive and more positive set of beliefs. Where could that take you? All experiences can be seen as opportunities to grow and develop spiritual awareness. Imagine holding the perception that whatever is happening is perfect. This view positions you to move in your chosen direction by way of your response to whatever is currently present. Coming from a place of total acceptance, with no blame or shame, speeds the healing and learning process and allows for a higher spiritual vibration. Hanging out in the idea that there is something wrong with you that needs fixing keeps you on the (⇓) side of the line, which is neither creative nor supportive. Re-patterning moves you to the (⇑) side of the line. The more you consciously practice, the more automatic the re-patterning becomes.

✳   ✳   ✳

Part II details each stage of the re-patterning process. There will be ample opportunity for you to consciously experience re-patterning as you learn it. As you practice, the process will move into your subconscious, and what you've re-patterned will become available to your conscious awareness. This interplay between the conscious and subconscious minds is fascinating to experience. You'll start discovering the places where your old patterns would run automatically, and a space will open for you to make a new, conscious decision. Keeping notes as you notice the changes in your behavior or responses to situations will further reinforce your learning. Your reflections and notes become your personal "owner's manual" as your subconscious and conscious minds learn to work together in a way that supports you in achieving what you want.

✳   ✳   ✳   ✳   ✳

Part 11

* * *

FLIPPING THE SWITCH

Chapter Three

UNCOVERING THE STRUCTURE:
What Makes Belief Re-patterning Work—Every Time

✳   ✳   ✳

"Leave the past and weave the path that leads to brighter times."

— EILEEN McGANN

Truly embracing and accepting who you really are is a journey to loving yourself. You can continue to hang on to the old ways, or you can leave the emotion that has held you in place and create your own pathway, enabling you to move forward with ease. As we've traveled to this point, you have laid some groundwork and begun to experience what happens when you train your mind to process information in this way. You've noticed that the focus is on the emotional tie to the belief and in connecting the (⇊) feeling to a (⇑) feeling. You discovered that the steps are incremental, and that you get feedback from your mind and body as you breathe in deeply and release the breath with each statement. Now it's time to look at the structure of re-patterning so that you consciously "weave the path" you wish to travel.

The boldfaced words in the series of Re-patterning Statements in each chapter indicate the six stages that are the framework of the technique. Regardless of how many statements are in any given series, there are always six basic steps in the structure of the Belief Re-patterning Statements:

1. Forgiveness

2. Permission

3. Choice

4. Freedom

5. Affirmation

6. Surrender

The steps are sequential but not hierarchical. One step leads naturally to the next, but no single one is more important than any other. They each have their unique perspective and purpose, their gifts and challenges. This chapter gives you an overview of the stages, and the following six chapters focus on the attributes of each step, including how it feels when you are beginning that step and how to move easily to the next. Like a staircase, the stages of re-patterning make it easier to move from a lower emotional vibration to a higher one. Jumping from a lower stairwell to the top landing just doesn't work, and neither does trying to go from a (⇓) feeling to a (⇑) feeling in one loud declaration.

When climbing stairs, you can take them one or two at a time. You can run up the stairs or use slow baby steps, depending on how sure you are of your footing and how quickly you need to move from where you are to where you want to be. If you're unsure, you can stay on the step where you're comfortable until you're certain of the next step; and if you run out of energy on the way up the stairs, you can stop and rest. When you trip, you can pick yourself up and start again. In between steps is a moment of uncertainty and imbalance, when your foot lifts from one to the next, but because the steps are close together and built to fit your stride, you move easily through the transition.

Defining the Steps

These incremental steps have a definite feeling and orientation, and this quick reference for each stage will be expanded on in the following chapters.

1. **Forgiveness** is the beginning of the Belief Repatterning process. Think of it as the lower stairwell of the staircase, where you may be feeling stuck. If you feel as if you *have to* or *don't want to,* you are at the entry point of the Forgiveness stage. You've been accepting and believing what your Inner Critic has to say. With Forgiveness Statements, your Inner Coach enters, encouraging you to move forward. This step is the point at which you acknowledge where you are. Forgiveness Statements are about letting go of the blame or shame that has kept you in the old ($\Downarrow$) energy, and initiating the process of change.

2. **Permission** involves becoming observant of your Inner Critic and leaving the (⇓) stuck place. With the help of your Inner Coach, you express the desire to take a step into new possibilities. There is a willingness to explore (⇑) options, and you invite yourself to move into something different. The energy around Permission is feeling as if you *want to,* even if you aren't sure *how to.*

3. **Choice** is the point where the two options, (⇓) and (⇑), are placed beside each other. Your Inner Critic and Inner Coach are in dialogue, examining the differences and making a conscious decision. As you enter this stage, the feeling is that of being on the fence, balancing between the two options, and then the tipping point occurs so that the decision is made. If you haven't yet moved into action but feel as if you *can,* you are ready for the Choice stage.

4. **Freedom** feels exciting and a bit like flying. Your Inner Coach is stretching its wings and trying on the new feeling. You experience all of the excitement of *I get to.* Your conscious mind is playing with the (⇑) feeling and imagining what it will create. This stage is about projecting that (⇑) feeling into the future and envisioning the actions you will take to create it.

5. In Belief Re-patterning, the term **Affirmation** is used in a very specific way. Unlike the common usage of the word to describe a positive statement that manifests something new, the Affirmation stage of Belief Re-patterning acknowledges where you have experienced

(⇑) in the past and connects the new feeling to specific, known experiences. In other words, this stage involves delving into your memory to identify the supportive feeling for the purpose of finding evidence to reinforce and expand it, and attract more of the same. At this stage you feel yourself anchoring the new belief with observations like, *I've done this before, Oh! I get it now,* or *That's like when I . . . ,* as your Inner Coach brings concrete examples from your past to your conscious awareness.

6. **Surrender** is the landing at the top of the staircase. You have arrived solidly at the (⇑) energy and begin to define yourself in this way. The energy is that of being grounded, and you are actively creating the new habit as your way of being. You hear yourself saying, *I am* (⇑) and believing it! The energy of the new emotion supports you in consciously creating your life and moving forward in a purposeful way.

Why the Steps Are Helpful

Events and experiences are neutral. It is your perceptions, based on your values, previous experiences, and learning, that translate those neutral events and color them to fit your current belief system. The foundation for many of your beliefs was laid in childhood and has been reinforced in your subconscious with experiences. Your conscious mind compares and contrasts the new information with what you hold to be true, and creates scenarios, explanations, and all kinds of interesting reasons to frame the new information to fit what you have stored in your subconscious mind. If you think of your subconscious mind as a series of file folders, each piece of new information that comes to your conscious mind needs to fit into one of those preexisting file folders; otherwise a new folder needs to be made. As with any good filing system, you first try to fit the new data into the existing files.

Building a new file takes effort, so we make do with the ones that we already have in place, bending and shaping the new information to fit our perceptions. Most of us are operating with parts of our filing system that were created when we were toddlers, and we haven't consciously reorganized or weeded those files, or created the new filing system for the changes we have experienced. We've just kept stuffing experiences into the existing files.

The Re-patterning Statements help you easily create new file folders in your subconscious based on supportive emotions. These files are placed higher in the priority sequence when new information comes to you, and begin to be filled quickly, proactively building the necessary beliefs that support your moving forward. The step-by-step process helps your mind sort this information into the new files. Your mind loves patterns because they can be run without conscious thought, and the Belief Re-patterning Statements provide those patterns.

To change your current reality and way of being in the world, you need to learn to think, feel, intuit, and sense differently. The more your subconscious mind can file your new, positive thoughts as patterns, the more efficiently you will manage change, and the more effectively you will manifest your desires into reality. The steps are so effective at moving this process to the subconscious that many of my clients and students report experiencing the Re-patterning Statements in their dreams!

How Does Belief Re-patterning Change Your Behavior?

Our behavior is always about playing out our current belief system. The excuses, explanations, and stories we create are based on our perceptions and are ways to keep our current beliefs in place.

You've used this powerful, creative storytelling feature of your mind to keep you firmly in an old pattern, but now you are shifting directions. Use your amazing storytelling capabilities to transform your belief system into one that supports your desired reality, by changing your behavior at the subconscious and conscious levels.

In this process the Forgiveness stage provides the opportunity for you to let go of blame, shame, and guilt around your behavior. Permission opens you to the possibility of creating different behavior based on a new way of being, and Choice is where you accept personal responsibility and consciously decide to have your actions come from the (⇑) side of the line from now on.

Your vision of your future is strengthened in the Freedom stage through giving your subconscious mind examples of what your behavior might be and how it will feel to have experiences from this new perspective. At the Affirmation stage you are consciously looking through old files to bring forth specific experiences and information to reinforce the new behavior that is creating your way of being. You then Surrender to this new way of being, affecting all your future thoughts, behaviors, actions, and experiences. You are now creating new results, the results you *want*.

What about Figuring Out What Happened?

As humans we spend a great deal of time and energy analyzing why things happen. Every moment spent wondering why something that we didn't like happened is a moment lost to creating something that we will enjoy.

Expending time and energy wondering, *Why did I do this? What was I thinking?* or *Why am I acting like this?* is crazy-making behavior. You did this because it reinforced the belief system you held in that moment. You may not be conscious of what part of that belief system was playing out; it may be a part that was patterned when you were 2, 3, or 12. Regardless, trying to find the source is counterproductive and will not get you where you want to be.

It really doesn't matter why you did or said anything you regret; instead, choose to hold a vision of how you would like things to be. You do not need to know the specifics of what the old belief was or of what your new reality will be. What works is identifying what feeling you no longer wish to experience (⇓) and what feeling you *do* wish to experience (⇑). Since beliefs are repetitive thoughts held in place by an emotion, when you change the emotion, you change the repetitive thoughts. Doing so shifts your beliefs, which changes your behavior, actions, and results. It is self-perpetuating, whether you are focusing on what you do or don't want, and it makes sense to focus on what you do want.

Quick Reflection:

THE OPPOSITE FEELING

You may be under the impression that you have to figure out what went wrong so that you don't repeat the same mistake. You may believe that you need to find the *source.* Think of all the time you've spent trying to sort all of that out. How do you feel about it? Stuck? As if your wheels are spinning? Frustrated? Go into that experience and list in your journal the unsupportive feelings. Mark these words as (⇓). Then draw a single line through the (⇓) emotion, with an arrow pointing to the right. Next to the tip of the arrow, write the (⇑) opposite feeling for you. It will look something like this:

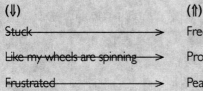

(⇓)	(⇑)
~~Stuck~~ ⟶	Free
~~Like my wheels are spinning~~ ⟶	Productive
~~Frustrated~~ ⟶	Peaceful

Choose the pair of words that, if re-patterned, you feel would really make a difference in your life. As you read these Re-patterning Statements out loud, insert your word pairing in the indicated blanks.

RE-PATTERNING STATEMENTS WITH YOUR WORD PAIRING

I **forgive** myself for believing that I need to keep feeling _____ (⇓).

I give myself **permission** to stop feeling _____ (⇓) and start feeling _____ (⇑).

I know how it feels to be _____ (⇓), and I know how it feels to be _____ (⇑); I **choose** _____ (⇑).

I am **free** to create _____ (⇑) feelings in my life.

I felt _____ (⇑) **when** I _____. *[Give a specific example; review Chapter 1, "Try This On! Practice: Focus on What You Love," for ideas.]*

I begin **defining myself as** _____ (⇑) from now on.

Since our words and behaviors come from a combination of our conscious and subconscious minds, having an automatic method for your subconscious mind to move your emotions to the supportive side of the line makes sense. All you need to do is be conscious of the emotion you are experiencing in the moment. If it's a (⇓) feeling, identify the opposite (⇑) feeling you want to have. You don't need to know the specifics of how you are going to get out of the (⇓) and achieve the (⇑); you simply need to identify and shift the emotion, which changes the thoughts and creates a new perception, developing a different belief, which *then* inspires new ideas and actions from a strong place of being.

You want to move in a purposeful direction. Even if you don't know exactly what that direction is, you can imagine how it will *feel*. Focus on changing the (⇓) feeling to the (⇑) feeling.

Have you ever been driving somewhere and all of a sudden realized you were lost? Trying to figure out why you got lost doesn't help. Your focus needs to be present with where you are, and then you can make a plan to get where you are going. You ask for directions from where you currently are. You don't start explaining how you backed out of your driveway and then took a left turn at the end of the street, describing all your moves up to where you became lost. That wouldn't make any sense at all. Instead you locate a signpost and consult a map, enter the coordinates into your GPS, or call your destination and say, "I am at the intersection of Crowchild Trail and Sarcee Trail heading north. How do I get to you from here?"

When you are physically lost and looking for directions, you know that it works to identify exactly where you are and move forward to where you are going, rather than to try to retrace your journey to figure out where you got lost. You focus your energy on where you are now and where you're going, rather than where you've been. The same principle works when you find yourself emotionally, mentally, or spiritually lost.

1. Identify the (⇓) feeling or the state of being you're experiencing that is not supportive of the direction you wish to go.

2. As quickly as possible, identify the positive opposite (⇑) of that feeling or state of being.

3. Let go of the need to analyze what happened or why it happened. It happened, and it's an opportunity for you to learn something different.

4. Using the two (⇓) and (⇑) words or phrases, re-pattern the belief using Re-patterning Statements.

Many clients want to know if something that is re-patterned will come back. The short answer is yes: re-patterning will not erase the memory, but it will release the emotional hook on the memory. The more complete answer is anything that you re-pattern may come back, but *not in the same way.* The (⇓) feelings and states of being you have re-patterned may return, usually when you are stressed, overtired, or hungry. They will not come back as automatically as they once did, because you have created the new neural pathways, and are building a more supportive belief system. The more you consciously practice being in the (⇑) feelings, the more you exercise the corresponding receptor cells and the less often the (⇓) feelings will occur. When you do experience the (⇓) feelings, you will notice that there is less intensity and that they last a much shorter time. This is because your subconscious will kick in with the linked (⇑) emotion and move you over to the supportive side of the line.

Try This One Practice::

CREATE FEELINGS THAT RAISE ENERGY

Practice creating the feelings that raise your own and others' energy, using this simple activity. Every time you move through a doorway from one space to another, inside or out, deliberately put a smile on your face! Do this consciously for a couple of hours. It's an easy habit to develop, and one that helps shift your vibration up and bring positive energy to whatever space you enter. Watch how others respond, and also notice how *you* feel. Reflecting on the new behavior will help reinforce it and move it into habit.

Because the Belief Re-patterning process is so deeply embedded in my way of being, people often ask me if I ever get angry or frustrated. Of course I do. All emotions are normal and healthy to experience. The difference is that instead of holding on to anger or experiencing frustration for days, weeks, months, years, or decades, I move through these emotions in moments, minutes, or hours. I spend more of my life experiencing (⇑) thoughts

and feelings, and when things don't seem to be working out, I re-pattern and create different results. As Belief
Re-patterning practitioner and Juno-nominated singer-
songwriter Eileen (**www.eileenmcgann.com**) urges in
the excerpt from her song "Pocketful of Rhymes" that
opens this chapter, you can also "leave the past and
weave the path that leads to brighter times" by learning
to re-pattern.

Beliefs come in groups and are woven together with
strong connections. Be gentle with yourself as you un-
ravel those old neural pathways that no longer work. Every belief you hold worked for you at one time; however,
if it's in the way or causing you pain, it no longer does.
We outgrow our beliefs, just as we outgrow clothing. An
outfit that looked cute when you were a child simply
doesn't fit anymore. That doesn't make the clothing
bad or wrong; it no longer serves you, so you let it go.
Imagine if you kept in your closet everything you had
ever worn. It would be so stuffed that there would be no
room for anything new. Similarly, some of your beliefs
are just hanging around from an earlier time and place
in your life. There's no need to make any of the beliefs or
feelings you are experiencing "wrong." They are there to
point you in the direction of what does fit and will work
for you now. As you release the old patterns, you will see
with clarity the new path you are weaving.

* * * * *

Chapter Four

FORGIVENESS:
The Doorway to Positive Thought

✳ ✳ ✳

*"True forgiveness is a willingness to
change your mind about your self."*

— ROBERT HOLDEN

Forgiveness is the foundation of change. You truly can
have anything you want; however, when you're har-
boring anger or jealousy, experiencing suffering or pain,
or living from a place of deficit or fear, what you want
is elusive. Once you're aware of the disconnection between where you are and what you want, you are ready
to enter into forgiveness.

Before your Inner Critic goes flying off the handle,
declaring, *I'm not forgiving them!* or *I can't forgive what
happened to me!* let me reassure you: with Belief Re-
patterning you are never required to forgive anyone else
for things that were said or done. Sometimes people do
horrible things to each other. This isn't about forgiving
others for wrongdoing; it's about forgiving yourself—for
believing that it was your fault, that you deserved what-

ever happened, or that you need to continue to be negatively affected. Self-forgiveness is the starting place for re-patterning your beliefs.

Forgiveness is:

- Recognizing the (⇓) and what it is doing to you

- Understanding that you have been stuck and deciding that you don't want to stay there

- Acknowledging that your emotions are coming from your perceptions

- Letting go of the need to be right

- Releasing the pain by removing the emotional charge

- Gaining control by identifying and naming the (⇓)

- The opportunity to leave the confines of victimhood

- Accepting yourself as a learner

- Stepping into personal responsibility for your life

- A loving act toward yourself

Forgiveness is *not:*

- Pretending that something didn't happen or that what happened doesn't matter

- Acting as if you are okay when you are not

- Accepting bad behavior from others

- Excusing wrongdoing by pretending that it's all right

- Allowing yourself to be a doormat

- Blaming yourself or beating yourself up

- Dismissing your feelings

You are ready for Forgiveness Statements when you are experiencing life in any of the following ways:

- Beating yourself up or feeling guilty over something you did or said

- Feeling undeserving or unworthy of good coming into your life

- Living in a state of fear over a situation

- Feeling lack or inadequacy about who you are

- Feeling defeated because you don't know how to make things better

- Operating from the deficit side of the line

- Feeling as if you are not being heard or acknowledged by others

- Yelling, arguing, fighting, or screaming

- Justifying your position, looking to place blame or fault

- Experiencing physical pain (which is your body trying to get your attention and bring awareness to what's happening)

- Feeling ready to be done with all of the (⇓)

What Happens at the Forgiveness Stage?

You've recognized that you are on *that side of the line,* and this stage begins the process of reconciling the belief that you need to stay in that uncomfortable space. Forgiveness Statements stop the downward spiraling and self-judgment you may be experiencing. When the rug gets pulled out from underneath you or you get a phone call that knocks the wind out of your sails, stating a simple Forgiveness Statement like *I forgive myself for believing that this needs to have control over me* will begin the process of getting you back on your feet.

Through self-forgiveness you recognize that the unsupportive place is not who you are, but is in fact pointing you toward what you want. When you hear yourself placing blame on anyone, yourself included, try: *I forgive myself for believing that this is who I am.* The belief that you need to be perfect is dispelled, and you begin to observe your reactions or behavior without moving yourself into shame or guilt. You enter the Forgiveness stage looking into the past from a perspective of what's wrong.

Forgiveness helps you let go of the *Oh no, look what I've done to myself!* point of view. You are ready to step out of the victim place and adopt an observant perspective. By forgiving yourself, you walk through fear, calming the chatter of your Inner Critic. The arrival of the compassionate and understanding Inner Coach helps clear your mind and opens the door for your thoughts to move to the possibilities of Permission.

Because your beliefs are a combination of your thoughts and emotions, the Forgiveness Statements are structured with *I forgive myself for believing . . . ,* rather than *I forgive myself for feeling, thinking, or doing . . .* The transformative power of forgiveness enters your heart: your body begins to relax, your mind becomes clearer, and your spirits lift. You may not know the answers to whatever you are facing, but the act of personal forgiveness brings welcome relief.

This stage focuses on self-forgiveness, yet through the re-patterning that occurs, you may find, as my client Angela did, that you want to extend that forgiveness to others:

> Belief Re-patterning has definitely been a process and an inner journey for me, helping me deal with my inner demons, and accept and forgive myself and others. It has opened my mind to the possibilities in all areas of my life and has taken me from being a very emotionally closed, shut-down individual who was always in protection mode to an open and willing participant in life and relationships. This tool has been a blessing for the past eight years, assisting me immensely in my spiritual and personal growth.

Angela initially came to me because she and her husband had been trying unsuccessfully to get pregnant for years. It's wonderful to have Angela bring her young daughter to see me now! Her ability to forgive herself ultimately led her to heal the emotional baggage she was carrying around her mother, and allowed her to open to the possibility of becoming a mother herself.

There is no need to push yourself to forgive others, but if you feel guided to include others in your Forgiveness Statements, you can personalize the statements by adding specific names (N). The first of the previous sample Forgiveness Statements could become: *I forgive myself for believing that the way things have been is the way they have to stay, and I ask _____ (N) to forgive me for believing that things between us can't change for the better.*

Remember, the purpose is to change your own thought patterns and beliefs, so the examples throughout the book focus on self-forgiveness. Depending on your spiritual beliefs, you may wish to include God, Universal Spirit, or any other higher power in your Forgiveness Statements. An example would be: *I forgive myself for believing that I don't deserve to nurture myself, and I ask God to forgive me for believing that I am undeserving.*

The Learning Process at the Forgiveness Stage

One of the ways we learn is through acknowledgment, and the Forgiveness Statements acknowledge where we are and that we want to make a change. This sends a powerful signal from the conscious mind to the subconscious mind. The statements interrupt the habit of looking backward from the deficit place, and create a disconnection in the previous neural pathway. The reticular activator is put on notice that a new belief is being created, and identifying the positive, opposite feeling before you begin the statements gives your RAS something real to focus on.

Your Inner Critic might respond to a Forgiveness Statement by insisting, *I didn't do anything wrong!* You're right. You didn't, or if you did, it's all right because you're learning to forgive yourself, and your Inner Coach can provide a supportive reply. You're opening your eyes to what is and being honest with yourself from an observant perspective. With practice, you stop seeing yourself as broken or a victim, and you welcome the comfort that this stage provides. It is the promise of a brighter place: even though you aren't there yet, you've opened the door. Your Inner Coach will begin to automatically bring Forgiveness Statements to your consciousness, providing emotional relief from any situation or circumstance. When you're moving through this stage, the ease that your body, mind, and soul experience feels like a warm blanket on a cold day or a splash of refreshing water on a hot one. As you incorporate Forgiveness Statements into your inner conversation, you'll move quickly from believing that you need to hang on to things that hurt you, including the unsupportive perceptions of others. Self-forgiveness allows you to breathe more deeply, and is a door that opens into a more supportive and positive space.

The Forgiveness Statements are important because they acknowledge how you're feeling and that the feeling is real. They let your Inner Critic know that it's not being pushed aside or ignored. The subconscious mind relaxes, because its message has been received: the Inner Critic has been heard, and you are paying attention. Rather than saying to yourself, *I shouldn't feel like this,* you are saying, *I feel this way, and I forgive myself for believing that I need to stay in this feeling.* Forgiveness keeps you out of the pretend *happy talk* place, and honors the truth of what you're feeling. When you feel honored, your mind is receptive to learning.

Your subconscious mind is designed to tightly hang on to anything you have learned. It will hang on to the old pattern until there is something more interesting that has a stronger emotion attached to it. The identification of the (⇑) feeling provides the impetus for the subconscious mind to let go of the old pattern and begin to create a new one, so you may want to include a Forgiveness Statement like *I forgive myself for believing that it is difficult to be calm in this situation.* You can incorporate both the (⇓) feeling and the (⇑) feeling by varying the structure of your Forgiveness Statements.

What about Mistakes?

How can you forgive yourself when you make a mistake? This story about how I developed a way to implement self-forgiveness in my classroom may shed some light on how *you* can re-pattern your thoughts around mistakes. The Re-patterning Statements work well to shift beliefs, but at school I needed to develop ways to re-pattern my students' language and actions that fit naturally into the classroom environment.

It was a Friday evening after a tough week of teaching. I felt as if I were out of sync, and decided to watch a movie to clear my mind and relax. At the end of the movie was a compilation of outtakes. I watched the actors stumble over their lines, repeating the same scene over and over until they got it right. There were no put-downs about what they had done wrong, just encouragement to try again and a lot of laughter. One of the scenes was finally deemed perfect at take 52! The directors showed the clapperboard operator marking all 52 takes. I was laughing so hard I had tears rolling down my face. My laughter lifted the heaviness I had been feeling, and I began thinking how I could have used several "takes" with some of the "scenes" that week in my classroom. The purpose of the clapperboard is to get the sound and visuals of a movie in sync during the editing process, and I knew that my words and actions were way out of sync with what I wanted. I had made a lot of mistakes that week.

A new way to re-pattern at school came to me. What if the culture of our classroom were the same as that movie set? What if mistakes were simply *missed takes?* I liked the idea and excitedly shared it with my students on Monday morning. Mistakes happen when our thoughts, words, and actions are out of sync with our surroundings. We agreed in our classroom to frame every mistake as a *missed take.* There was always the opportunity, just as on a film set, for another *take.*

Mistakes don't define us; they are an invitation to try again, to get our thoughts and actions in sync with each other and with what we are trying to accomplish. They are a natural part of the learning process. Most of the mistakes we experience are what I call "honest mistakes." There's no malice or negative intent; the detours and false starts are part of coming to understand something new.

The most damaging aspect of most mistakes is the way we put ourselves down and beat ourselves up after we make them. In our classroom we shifted the emotion around them by seeing them as missed takes. This became part of the way we spoke in the classroom, encouraging each other to do take *two, three,* or *four*—whatever number it took to achieve what we needed. One of the students created a poster for the front of the room: "Mistake = Missed Take."

Hit the Rewind Button

Another concept that became common in our classroom was *rewind.* With a push of a button on a tape recorder, you can back up, erase what was said, and rerecord. My students loved having their own *rewind* buttons so that they could back up and try again. Whenever students put themselves down, their classmates would draw their attention to it with the word *rewind.* They were then encouraged to say what they needed to say from a supportive place. Similarly, if during group work, one of the students said something in a harsh or hurtful way, the group asked that person to rewind.

Everyone learned that how something is said often gets in the way of the message. The students realized that how they spoke to themselves would spill out onto others. They became more respectful with their self-talk and, in turn, with their classmates. The simple implementation of *rewind* brought awareness to the way they expressed themselves, providing them the opportunity to hear what they were saying and do another *take.* Within days, students were monitoring themselves midsentence and would frequently say, "Rewind. What I meant to say was . . ." I have since introduced the *rewind* and *missed takes* concepts into corporate and business environments with equal success.

You have your very own *rewind* button to use whenever your Inner Critic surfaces. Rewind is a conscious decision to re-pattern and ask your Inner Coach to step up. You can do this on your own, and it is also a great practice to introduce in a family setting or with a close friend or partner. Speaking gently to yourself and others raises your vibration and changes your outcomes.

RE-PATTERNING STATEMENTS FOR MISSED TAKES

I **forgive** myself for believing that those old mistakes define me.

I give myself **permission** to consider mistakes as missed takes.

I **choose** to encourage my learning through "rewind"!

I'm **free** to learn from my previous takes, rewind, and move forward.

Every experience is an opportunity for me to learn and grow.

I **am** learning and moving forward.

What if you simply began seeing the times you are out of sync as missed takes? Could you imagine the relief you would feel in knowing that you could just have a do-over? Some situations, like our classroom environment, allowed for missed takes and rewinds. But sometimes the opportunity to rewind just doesn't exist, and that's when your Inner Critic can really take over, unless you develop an automatic way for your Inner Coach to support you.

Try This One! Practice:

FOCUS ON POSITIVE BEHAVIOR

In my teaching practice, I learned to bring awareness to students' inappropriate behavior by focusing on building their positive self-image and making a plan for next time. When a student messed up, I would bring awareness to the situation by saying, "Josh, that's not like you; what would you do next time?" or "That's not the Marilee I know. What might work better?" This was a great way for students to learn from their mistakes, but it was still teacher directed. I wanted my students to be empowered and able to build themselves up when they stumbled.

I experimented with myself and tried turning the comment inward. Whenever I did something I wasn't happy about and my Inner Critic would start with the *shoulda, coulda, woulda* treatment, I would consciously bring my Inner Coach into the conversation and say to myself in my most empathetic teacher voice, *That's not like me; next time I'll* _____. I filled in the blank with what my Inner Critic was telling me I *shoulda, coulda, woulda* done differently. If my Inner Critic said, *You should have thought about that before you did it,* I'd switch to my Inner Coach: *That's not like me; next time I'll think before I do.* When my Inner Critic started beating me up with *You could have seen that coming!* my Inner Coach would step in with *That's not the Suze I know. Next time I'll be more aware of what's happening around me.*

This simple habit worked like a Forgiveness Statement, so I brought it to my classroom: *That's not like me; next time I'll* _____. The kids grabbed on to it and began making empowering plans for next time instead of beating themselves up over last time. Try this when *you* find yourself *shoulda, coulda, woulda*–ing yourself!

Whether you use a direct Forgiveness Statement, start viewing mistakes as missed takes, hit the rewind button, or begin making a plan for next time, the intention is the same: you are releasing the emotional hook that pulls your energy down. You are engaging in a conscious dialogue that moves you away from damaging, self-destructive thoughts. Let go of the shame, blame, guilt, and pain. You did the best you knew how to do at the time. You know how to encourage those you care about when they are feeling down. Are you ready to treat yourself the same way?

Quick Reflection:

HONOR YOURSELF

In your journal, identify a compassionate and honoring conversation you've had with someone. Can you imagine being as compassionate and honoring with yourself? What would happen if you were kinder and gentler with yourself?

The Transition from Forgiveness to Permission

Through the Forgiveness Statements you move from avoidance to acknowledgment and take personal responsibility for your response without beating yourself up. You recognize that it's all perception, and are willing to change yours so that you can feel better. The Inner Critic and the Inner Coach have entered into a conversation to address the imbalance you're feeling. Forgiveness is about letting go of the pain and releasing the emotional charge of the old pattern. The transition into Permission means getting past the way you've been defining yourself and into the image of who you may become through this experience. You are no longer being held hostage by anyone or anything, including your own unsupportive emotions. You are consciously creating your reality by releasing old perceptions and beginning the process of adopting a more positive point of view by increasing supportive emotions.

Self-forgiveness is a habit worth developing. If your previous habits involved beating yourself up or putting yourself down, decide to routinely acknowledge where you are and release the need to stay there. Forgiveness is the decision to flip the switch, change the way things have been, and let go of the things that have dragged you down and worn you out. It's a decision to reclaim your personal power from the people and experiences that have caused you pain until now. The Belief Re-patterning stage of Forgiveness is an invitation from your Inner Coach to begin a supportive inner conversation. Having opened the door through Forgiveness, you are now ready to explore the possibilities through Permission.

* * * * *

Chapter Five

PERMISSION:
Opening to Possibilities

✳   ✳   ✳

"We first make our habits, and then our habits make us."
— ATTRIBUTED TO JOHN DRYDEN

Permission is a step in the direction of creating what you want. You've engaged your Inner Coach through the act of self-forgiveness. The possibilities and potential begin to emerge from the fog you were in while your attention was on the *problem* or what you *should do* about the situation. Through this stage you reclaim your creative power and use it to grow a new belief. You shift your attitude by giving yourself permission to have a different feeling, and that changes your perception, which changes the experience. By doing this, you allow yourself to "deserve," give yourself value, and begin honoring yourself and your needs. This part of the re-patterning process is where you consider accepting positive emotions.

If forgiveness is about letting go of the emotion that has limited you, permission is the space of letting go of the overwhelming details of how you will create whatever it is you want to manifest. You come to the understanding that your role is to create the (⇑) feeling. Once you are consciously moving toward the supportive emotional state, all the necessary details and the inspired action will come. Permission is about allowing yourself to release the (⇓) feeling and consider claiming the (⇑) way of being from now on.

Care for yourself enough by giving yourself the go-ahead to feel how you want to feel. The simple action of allowing the emotion of what you want, need, or desire opens you up to receiving it. Permission to experience the feeling you want allows you to let go of the unsupportive feelings that have, until now, blocked your desires. Giving yourself permission is a declaration: *I am ready and willing.*

Permission is:

- Invitational

- An outward, future orientation to your thoughts

- An opportunity to learn and grow from wherever you find yourself

- Declaring what you'd like to feel or experience in your life

- Forward moving

- A recognition of what supports you

- The introduction of potential

- The engaging of competency and creativity

- An expansion of possibilities

Permission is *not:*

- Getting the go-ahead from anyone else

- Talking yourself into something you aren't ready for or don't want

- Trying to figure out how to do something

- Wondering what others want you to do

- Dwelling in the shoulds, musts, or have-tos

You are ready for Permission Statements when you are experiencing life in any of the following ways. You are:

- Tentative, maybe even a bit scared, but know it is right for you

- Wishing you had said or done something you didn't

- Feeling the fear and wanting to do it anyway

- Ready to strengthen your wings

- Going into the unknown and wanting some support

- Ready to remind yourself of who you really are

- Prepared to grow and learn something new

- Looking for advice, confirmation, validation, or answers outside of yourself

- Not quite ready to take personal responsibility but moving in that direction

What Happens at the Permission Stage?

There are wonderful people, exciting opportunities, and interesting events coming your way all the time. If you aren't experiencing life in this way, this is your chance to strengthen your Inner Coach and put on your catcher's mitt. Permission is the place of learning to receive. Many of us are conscious about giving our best to others, but when it comes to accepting it into our lives, we often unconsciously deflect the good with our old patterns of feeling not good enough, unworthy, or undeserving. The Permission stage exercises our ability to receive with grace and ease.

As you begin re-patterning, your Inner Critic may bring up all kinds of objections. Respond to a *You can't do that!* objection with a Permission Statement like *I give myself permission to change and be* _____ (⇑). If the objection continues to be strong, step back into Forgiveness and consciously acknowledge the objection with something like, *I forgive myself for believing that I can't, and I now give myself permission to move forward with* _____ (⇑). Gently work with the messages from your Inner Critic until the Inner Coach becomes stronger. Pushing your Inner Critic aside or getting frustrated by its comments is counterproductive and will send you back into the (⇓). By engaging both the Inner Critic and Inner Coach, you will receive a great deal of helpful information about your belief system that you can then use to make the general Re-patterning Statements specific to you.

"Flip Your Switch from Inner Critic to Inner Coach" is the introductory Belief Re-patterning course I offer in various locations, as well as online. During a recent course held in Edmonton, Alberta, I met Joseph. Physically challenged, Joseph relies on a motorized wheelchair for mobility. He is an incredible individual who has studied Reiki to keep his energy moving within his body, and he keeps his brilliant mind stimulated. At the beginning of the course, I ask participants to share what brought them to the class. Joseph eloquently said, "Belief Re-patterning has changed my life. I no longer feel overwhelmed. Finally, there's an easy way to eliminate the negative mental chatter. If I can give myself permission to feel bad, then I can definitely give myself permission to feel good." His observations quieted the class as we all looked within, wondering what we could give ourselves permission to feel.

Often we look outside of ourselves to raise our spirits or solve our challenges. As your Inner Coach is strengthened and learns to give you the permission you seek, you begin to step into your personal power. At first you may be tentative, but as you practice allowing good into your life, you will come to see that there is enough abundance for all and you are willing to claim your good.

It's as though a door to a hallway has been opened, and the Permission Statements are the night-light that dispels the darkness so that you can keep moving toward your dreams and desires. At this stage you become willing to receive and explore what you want to experience. You feel yourself breathing more deeply, and your mind moves from the past focus of the Forgiveness Statements to a future orientation as you give yourself permission to let go of what no longer serves you, as well as permission to claim what does. Permission excites the courage of your heart, and sparks creativity and movement into the mind-set where new plans come easily.

The only person to whom you can truly give permission is *you*. If you feel guided to include others in your statements, you can do so; however, the effectiveness of the Permission Statements lies in claiming personal power, so the focus remains on you. For example, you could personalize the statement *I give myself permission to value myself by acknowledging my accomplishments, both large and small* by adding . . . *and I am open to receiving the acknowledgment of my partner and boss with ease.* This is much more effective than simply stating, *I give my partner and boss permission to value me by acknowledging my accomplishments.* In that example you are giving your personal power away to your partner and your boss. Permission Statements open you up to receive, but not rely on, the energy of others. You may also wish to enhance a statement like *I give myself permission to nurture myself daily* by adding your spiritual beliefs: . . . *and I give myself permission to be guided by my higher power in nurturing myself.*

When the students in my Belief Re-patterning courses begin creating their own statements, they sometimes
get hung up on identifying their emotions. When I ask,
"What do you want instead?" inevitably the response is, "I
don't want . . ." For example, if they are feeling frustrated
and I ask them what they want instead, the response is frequently "I don't want to be frustrated." I'll often respond
then with, "If you no longer felt frustrated, what would
the feeling be?" The identification of the opposite feeling, framed in supportive language, is the crux of the Permission stage. Say each of the following statements, and
breathe in after each one. Feel the difference in your body:

I want to feel calm and centered.
I don't want to be frustrated.

Notice how the two statements create quite different
physical responses. The first one moves your energy up,
and the second one pulls you down, referring back to
the feeling of frustration. It's important to identify feelings that lift your energy up, and using the (⇑) can give
a visual clue and reinforcement.

If someone is feeling financially strapped, that person might answer, "I want less stress around money."
This may seem to be a (⇑) response, but the focus remains on stress. I then ask, "If you were less stressed
about money, how would you feel?" It might be *secure,*
solid, free, content, or any number of emotions that truly
lift the person's energy. The opposite, uplifting emotion
will be different depending on the situation and the individual. For some, the opposite of *lonely* might be *con-*
nected; for others, *loved, welcomed,* or *included* would be

the focus of the re-patterning. It is highly individualized and changes according to circumstances.

When I work with a client, I use muscle testing as the tool to identify both the (⇓) and (⇑) words. Muscle testing, also known as *kinesthetic testing,* is a recognized way of tapping into the body's wisdom and knowledge, providing a different perspective, often, from what the mind thinks is happening. Muscle testing is an effective means of identifying what your body holds as its truth. Your body speaks in the language of feeling and emotion, and I discovered that I could use muscle testing as a tool to identify the exact emotion in question. There is a huge body of work around kinesthetic testing, and if you are curious, you can easily research it on the Internet. I teach simple muscle testing in my "Flip Your Switch from Inner Critic to Inner Coach" course, but for your personal re-patterning, use the simple method of determining a yes and a no response that you've been practicing by *feeling into* your mind and body's responses, and noticing whether your energy moves (⇓) or (⇑).

Try This One! Practice:

CREATE OPPOSITES

To support the identification of both the (⇓) block and the (⇑) emotion, I created the 62-page book *Path-Ways to Patterns: A Guide for Belief Re-patterning.* Available for purchase from the website (**beliefrepatterning .com**), it is an alphabetical listing of feelings that assists in not only naming, but also linking, the emotions you want to move away from (⇓) with those you want to increase (⇑). Although you only use one or sometimes two of the (⇑) words in any Re-patterning Statement series, having more supportive possibilities helps open your mind to what you *really* want instead. Simply practicing the activity of building opposites strengthens the neural pathways and supports your Inner Coach.

Here are a few samples from *PathWays to Patterns* to get you started:

(⇓)		(⇑)
Hampered	⇒	Supported, nurtured, believed, encouraged
Less than	⇒	Equal to, valued, respected, contributing
Tired	⇒	Energized, rested, enthusiastic, fulfilled, alert, alive
Uncertain	⇒	Decisive, sure, purposeful, knowing, committed

List these emotions in your journal and write some (⇑) opposite feelings for each (⇓).

(⇓)		(⇑)
Angry	⇒	
Not good enough	⇒	
Worried	⇒	
Reluctant	⇒	
Sad	⇒	
Taken for granted	⇒	

A great activity to do during your day is to observe others and, in your mind, name the emotion you are witnessing. For example, if you see a co-worker being *short-tempered,* think of the opposite, positive feelings: *even-tempered, centered, grounded,* or *calm.* Reinforce the opposite in your mind with a Permission Statement like *I know what it's like to be short-tempered, and I know what it's like to be grounded and calm. I give myself **permission** to be grounded and calm.*

You can also do this linking while watching TV. During a commercial break, name the emotions the characters are showing. If it's an (⇓) emotion, think of opposite (⇑) emotions. If it is an (⇑) emotion, expand it. For example, if a character in a TV show is *happy,* remember a time when you felt happy, and then explore similar (⇑) emotions, like *excited, thrilled, upbeat.* Expanding your vocabulary of (⇑) emotions supports your Inner Coach, and learning to pinpoint the exact emotion will make your re-patterning more efficient. The identification of the *moving toward* word is as personal as how you like your coffee or the toppings on your pizza. You know exactly how you like it, and at this stage, you give yourself permission to have *exactly* the emotion you want.

You may not have felt that you've had permission from others in the past; however, as an adult you have the power to offer it to yourself. This is your life and your creation, and the Permission stage is one of recognizing and exercising personal empowerment. You'll know that you have moved your thoughts to the Choice stage when you are ready to move from possibility into action.

The Learning Process at the Permission Stage

"Any idea that is held in the mind, emphasized, feared, or reverenced begins at once to clothe itself in the most convenient and appropriate physical form that is available."

— NAPOLEON HILL

Permission Statements begin to shift the reticular activator to allow information into the conscious mind that answers the question *What do I want instead?* Remember, your reticular activator focuses on whatever is considered relevant. The Permission stage consists of quite literally instructing your RAS to scan all incoming information from your environment for opportunities to experience (⇑) feelings. You are opening your eyes to what could be by allowing yourself the possibility of feeling how you want to feel. Instead of leaving you to look outward to others for validation, the Permission Statements help your conscious mind realize that it is *you* who can give yourself all the permission you need. You then are consciously instructing your subconscious mind to access the files that are (⇑).

Giving yourself permission awakens your personal power, and because it feeds the creative part of your mind, this is the stage that may begin to surface in your dreams as your subconscious sorts through old patterns while you sleep. You may find yourself coming to a brief moment of awareness in the middle of the night and hear your Inner Coach say, *I give myself permission to . . .* as you roll over and go back to sleep.

If you are short on time or aren't in a situation where you can give conscious attention to your re-patterning, simply giving yourself permission to entertain the positive feeling or explore the possibility of inhabiting the (⇑) state of being will spur your subconscious mind to work on the idea while you go about your day. Permission sets the direction your mind will take. If you're feeling really challenged to re-pattern, say a couple of (⇑) Permission Statements before you go to bed and ask your mind to work on them while you sleep. Check in with yourself the next morning, and you will discover that your subconscious mind has processed most, if not all, of the re-patterning.

Identifying what you would rather feel begins to focus the reticular activator and stops the mind from spiraling into the old pattern. The Permission Statements set the intention, raise the level of your vibration, and get more of the (⇑) energy flowing in your direction.

It's Like Planting a Garden

I run my practice from my home. Outside my office door is an 8-by-12-foot garden. When my partner and I moved here several years ago, the garden plot was full of weeds. Thistles, crabgrass, and dandelions had choked out anything that might have once been planted there. We moved too late in the season to plant but did spend a great deal of time pulling weeds. A few weeks later, it was overgrown again. By spring it looked as it had when we first arrived. The weeds were pulled again and again. The yard needed a lot of work, and we just didn't get around to planting a garden that year either. The patch was an eyesore as we tried unsuccessfully to keep up with the weeds.

Over the next winter we committed to planting a garden in the spring. When the warm weather arrived, we bought seeds, weeded yet again, and planted a variety of vegetables. We didn't put any additional effort into the garden, letting the rain water it over the summer. The lettuce came up first, and we enjoyed several meals of fresh greens. There were weeds but not very many. The harvest wasn't bountiful and some of the vegetables never matured, but we had a garden.

Last spring I looked out in amazement. Even though the snow was gone, the garden area was dark brown with a few tiny weeds. It was as if the earth knew its purpose and was patiently waiting for us to set our intention and plant the seeds we wished to nurture and harvest for the year.

Your mind is like a garden plot. If you've neglected it, it will be filled with the weeds of negative thoughts. Some will be strong, with deep, intertwining root systems. If you focus on pulling weeds, more will grow in to replace those you've pulled. However, by consciously focusing on how you want to feel, you plant the seeds of intention that will provide you with the harvest you desire. When you tend to your mind by giving yourself permission to move your thoughts to the (⇑) side of the line, you provide the nourishing environment for those supportive beliefs to grow strong.

Gratitude and daily practice provide the rain and sunshine for those beliefs to mature and bring your desired results. When you plant a garden, you don't know exactly what your yield will be, and watching the plants grow and develop is part of the process. When you plant (⇑) feelings in your mind by giving yourself permission, you do not know how those feelings will grow and develop. You have simply placed new possibilities in your mind, just as the seeds are the possibilities in the garden.

You'll observe the growth of your positive belief system through the re-patterning process. And just as with a garden, you can plant something different next time, while continuing to cultivate what supports and nurtures you now!

The Need for Perfection

One of the most destructive perceptions many people hold is the need for perfection. Somewhere along the line, they come to believe that they have to be perfect, and they either knock themselves out trying or give up in the process. They focus on their mistakes and flaws, and the Inner Critic runs wild.

The need for perfection closes off positive energy flow. Permission Statements open you to possibility. Most of us harbor some kind of perfectionism. You've likely held yourself back from something because you didn't think you were good enough to do it right. The belief that you need to be perfect or do things perfectly steals dreams and allows you to settle for less than is available to you. Give yourself permission to release the need for perfection in your life.

RE-PATTERNING STATEMENTS FOR RELEASING PERFECTIONISM

I **forgive** myself for believing that I have to be perfect.

I **forgive** myself for believing that I have to know how to do it all before I start.

I give myself **permission** to recognize that I am here to learn and to grow.

I give myself **permission** to release the need for perfection.

I can hang on to the need for perfection, or I can learn and grow. I **choose** to learn and grow.

I **choose** to let go of the need for perfection; that old belief has held me back long enough.

I am **free** to learn and grow.

I am **free** to find the perfection right where I am.

When I learned to drive, I wasn't perfect, but I **learned** along the way.

I like learning something new; it **happened when** I _____ [example].

I **see myself** learning and growing, and it feels right.

I **am** perfectly positioned to learn what I need to learn in order to grow in the direction of my dreams.

When you let go of the need for perfection, you stop allowing your Inner Critic to define you. Listening to your *inner conversations* from an observant place will provide great insight into the beliefs you carry about yourself. Make a note in your journal of any message your Inner Critic or Inner Coach brings forth as you say the Re-patterning Statements out loud. Usually these messages come to mind in the space while you are breathing in and out. You are perfectly positioned to learn and grow, and the more re-patterning you do, the more clearly you'll see the perfection that is already present in you.

A colleague tacked a handwritten copy of "The Rose" on my bulletin board 25 years ago. I've treasured this excerpt from Timothy Gallwey's book *The Inner Game of Tennis* (Random House, 2008), and used it as a touchstone for myself and my students with respect to giving ourselves permission to see ourselves as perfect, right now, right where we are.

> When we plant a rose seed in the earth, we notice that it is small, but we do not criticize it as "rootless and stemless." We treat it as a seed, giving it the water and nourishment required of a seed. When it first shoots up out of the earth, we don't condemn it as immature and underdeveloped; nor do we criticize the buds for not being open when they appear. We stand in wonder at the process taking place and give the plant the care it needs at each stage of its development. The rose is a rose from the time it is a seed to the time it dies. Within it, at all times, it contains its whole potential. It seems to be constantly in the process of change; yet at each state, at each moment, it is perfectly all right as it is.

> ## Quick Reflection:
>
> ## GIVE YOURSELF PERMISSION
>
> What do you give yourself permission to be? The details will become clear once the intention is set: What do you really want? How will you feel when that happens?
>
> Set your intention for the way you want to feel, and write from that perspective. Create a list in your journal of (⇑) emotions that you would like to be defined by, and then give yourself permission to practice those (⇑) feelings, creating the habit so they become your normal way of being.

The Transition from Permission to Choice

Through the Permission Statements you move from feeling tentative to developing enough courage to approach the line that divides your thoughts into supportive and unsupportive. Permission builds nurturing and caring feelings toward yourself, and gives you the needed security to consider stepping over that line at the Choice stage. You are learning to be your own best friend, parent, or coach by connecting to who you really are and giving voice to your truth. Focusing on the uplifting emotions provides the incentive for change and speeds up the learning process.

We each have an inner thermostat that regulates what emotions we are comfortable experiencing as our norm. The Permission Statements readjust this inner thermostat, setting it to a higher vibrational level, and we then choose it as our norm at the next stage of the re-patterning process.

As you move through Permission into Choice, your Inner Coach will become predominant, and when your Inner Critic does appear, it will be less harsh and judgmental. Your Inner Coach will begin giving you continual positive messages to reinforce the new perception you are patterning into your subconscious.

Permission opens your mind to the possibility of something better occurring in the future. The specifics of that future will come from the feelings you're consciously creating.

* * * * *

Chapter Six

CHOICE:
Making a Conscious Decision

✳ ✳ ✳

"We need to teach the next generation of children from day one that they are responsible for their lives. Mankind's greatest gift, also its greatest curse, is that we have free choice. We can make our choices built from love or from fear."

— ATTRIBUTED TO ELISABETH KÜBLER-ROSS

Children are sponges, soaking up beliefs and perceptions. Wired to learn, each of us adopted whatever information and beliefs were available, because we were unaware of other options. With the perspective of maturity, we make personal decisions about what fits for us and what doesn't.

As you move through your life, you become a different person with different needs, so it follows that you make different choices. This stage involves sorting your emotions into what you are strengthening and what you are releasing. *You* are the only one who can make these choices for you.

Your Inner Critic and Inner Coach have moved from a tug-of-war, and are now engaged in a productive back-and-forth conversation. You call into question the choices that were made for you that you adopted as a child. You elect to honor yourself and your parents by holding on to the beliefs they passed to you that support you in your current reality. You further honor yourself by letting go of the ones that do not serve you and are in the way of your growth, even if they worked for your parents in their time and place, and may have worked for you until now.

Every one of us is unique and has personal preferences about everything from how much cream we like in our coffee, to how we want to experience our lives. If we're not satisfied with something, we can't always change the situation, but we always have the choice to change our perception and feel differently. Many of us hold ourselves back because we are afraid of making the *wrong* choice.

Think of your choices as deciding on a color of paint to use. Pick a color and try it. The paint colors your perception: if the perception works and is supportive, keep painting with it. If you find that your choice isn't serving you, put that paintbrush down, pick another one up, and keep painting. Sitting and staring at a blank canvas because you can't decide which color to use will not create a work of art. Waiting for someone else to hand you a brush dipped in a color he or she has chosen before you get started will likely lead to frustration and resentment down the road. Only you can choose the perception that will serve you, and then integrate that perception into the habits that will support you in creating the work of art that is your life.

In your Choice Statements you are not choosing what to *do;* you are choosing how to *be.* If an action is obvious, include it, but keep the focus on the emotion. Choose an (⇑) emotion and use the power of your conscious mind in the present moment to concentrate on that feeling. It is your decision to define your experience; no one else has that power. You set your intention to embrace who you really are and how you respond to any person, situation, or circumstance.

Choice is:

- Being in the present moment

- Weighing the (⇓) and (⇑) options

- A crossroads or tipping point of change

- Declaring a direction

- Stating your clear intention and moving toward it

- A conscious decision

- Stepping over the line to the supportive side

- Personal and individualized

- Empowering and personally gratifying

Choice is *not:*

- Forcing yourself or being pushed into something

- Made for you by circumstances

- Uncomfortable or scary

- Made by you for someone else, including your children, partner, or parents

- What you think you should choose to make someone else happy

- About the details of how, what, when, or where

You are ready for Choice Statements when you are experiencing life in any of the following ways:

- On the fence and wavering between two or more options

- Wondering which way to go or what to do

- Wanting change and willing to create new habits

- Welcoming the new learning

- Finding that what you are thinking about is new and a bit exciting

- Feeling solid in your resolve to experience life differently

- Experiencing relief around something that had you upset or confused

What Happens at the Choice Stage?

You've experienced turning points in your life, where everything changed because you shifted your understanding by arriving at a new awareness. The Choice Statements are the point in the Belief Re-patterning technique where the switch is actually flipped. Forgiveness and Permission have allowed you to arrive at the place where you are ready to make a decision. The clarity that comes with declaring Choice Statements gives you the ability to emotionally and energetically step over the line to supportive thought.

How you define yourself and what you want to include or embrace in your life is the result of the decisions you make moment to moment. Re-patterning allows you to remove the subconscious choices that haven't been working for you and replace them with conscious choices about how you truly want things to be from now on. Renowned psychiatrist Viktor Frankl, a Holocaust survivor, made this point abundantly clear in *Man's Search for Meaning* (Simon & Schuster, 1984): ". . . everything can be taken from a man but one thing: the last of the human freedoms—to choose one's attitude in any given set of circumstances, to choose one's own way." In the past it may have seemed as if circumstances controlled your attitude, but part of becoming self-aware is recognizing that you choose your attitude at all times, independent of circumstances.

Brenda, a Belief Re-patterning practitioner, stayed with me the week her father died. The morning of the funeral we did some re-patterning to support her. She knows the power of the simple daily exercise (which you'll learn in Chapter 15) of choosing a word for the day. Her (⇑) word that came up that day was *joyful*. She looked at me with disbelief in her eyes, but said, "I trust this process, and I will trust the word."

I gave her a hug, and we both knew that somehow the feeling of joy would sustain her when she made the choice to experience that feeling. That evening, when she returned to my home, I expected her to arrive feeling tired after a tough day; instead she was vibrant and energized. She told me how she'd asked everyone at the gathering to relate a joyful experience they'd had with her father. She focused her mind and chose to experience her father's life as *joyful,* and this emotion spread throughout the gathering.

With the new ideas that begin coming to your consciousness at the Choice stage, you can begin to address *How will I do that?*—the crazy-making question that may have kept you stuck. However, just as Brenda's experience illustrates, this stage requires trust. The decision point of Choice involves faith and a degree of belief in yourself in (⇑) the moment. The empowering Permission Statements nudge you to take a step into the unknown, trusting that what you need and the way to make it happen will appear. This is the stage of the re-patterning process where you exercise personal will. Learning to make your choices from the (⇑) side of the line is powerful.

Can you imagine choosing how you want to be in any given set of circumstances? Rather than just *seeing how it goes,* focusing your mind on an (⇑) emotion, and making a conscious decision to experience it, increases your ability to proactively create the results you desire in potentially challenging situations.

Quick Reflection:

WHAT IS YOUR CHOICE?

Pick a specific example (S) of something you want that you have had challenges attaining in the past. It may be a loving partner, financial freedom, a healed relationship with a family member, a positive outcome to a community project, or anything else you desire. How do you currently feel about that? Select one or two words to capture the (⇓) feeling of not yet achieving what you desire. How will you feel when this is resolved? Distill those feelings into one or two (⇑) words, remembering that you don't have to figure out *how* to feel (⇑) in the current situation.

Your job in this reflection is simply to identify what you're currently feeling and what the (⇑) opposite of that feeling is. Let go of the *when, where, why,* or *how.* We will address those, but at the Choice stage of re-patterning, you are simply recognizing how you do feel (⇓) about the situation and making a conscious decision about how you want to feel (⇑).

Write down the words in your journal, and place the up and down arrows beside them. Also jot down a time when you felt (⇑) in the past (P). The following Re-patterning Statements become specific and personalized as you insert both the (⇓) and (⇑) feelings you identified, as well as the specific situation (S).

RE-PATTERNING STATEMENTS
FOR CONSCIOUS DECISION

I **forgive** myself for believing that I need to stay stuck in the feeling of _____ (⇓) when I think about _____ (S). I'm tired of feeling _____ (⇓).

I give myself **permission** to let go of feeling _____ (⇓) and allow myself to feel _____ (⇑).

I can feel _____ (⇓), or I can feel _____ (⇑); I **choose** to feel _____ (⇑).

I am **free** to bring _____ (⇑) to my thoughts about _____ (S).

I've **experienced** the feeling of _____ (⇑) before when I _____ (P).

I **am** consciously bringing _____ (⇑) to my thoughts about _____ (S).

The Learning Process at the Choice Stage

During the Choice stage, you consciously connect the (⇓) emotions with the (⇑) ones and give clear direction to your subconscious to prioritize the supportive feeling. One of the ways in which we learn is through comparing and contrasting. By placing the two opposite feelings together, your conscious, logical mind will decide that it makes sense to go with the (⇑) feeling whenever you have a choice. This decision is then stored subconsciously. When your Inner Critic calls forth information, it does so by sorting through the files stored in your subconscious and bringing to your conscious awareness whatever has the greatest emotional charge or connection.

Practicing the first three stages of Belief Re-patterning (Forgiveness, Permission, and Choice) trains your mind to move easily from (⇓) emotions to (⇑) ones. If your Inner Critic insists, *But it's always like this,* your Inner Coach can intercede and reframe whatever is happening in a supportive manner. Your Inner Coach has the skills to reply, *I forgive myself for believing that the way things have been is the way they have to stay, I give myself permission to change,* or *That's the way it was, and from now on, I choose to . . .* You are the one who chooses which emotions to increase, and which to release, to create the perceptions and beliefs that support you.

One of the most profound choices you can make is to allow your learning to come easily. If you are a graduate of the school of hard knocks, develop the belief that you've already done the hard part and that from here on, you will learn easily. Choice Statements actually disconnect the old emotional hooks from the beliefs. You develop who you really are by strengthening the things that you like about yourself and learning from the things that create discomfort for you. Any new habit or learning may feel awkward at first, simply because it's different from what you're used to. If you want change in your life, you'll need to step into some unknown places, and the Choice Statements are the entry points.

I learned a great practical illustration of this choice point from Dave, a friend who is an art instructor at a local college. When he is encouraging his students to stretch their perceptions and they're resistant to change, he speaks of the *territory of unknowing*. This is whatever is outside of your comfort zone, something that is unusual or different from what you're accustomed to. Your body goes on alert whenever something is unfamiliar. All your senses are heightened, and you can move easily into fear. To help his college students understand the territory of unknowing, Dave uses a simple exercise. Try it yourself right now:

1. Fold your hands in your lap in the same way you did on your desk when your first- or second-grade teacher wanted your attention.

2. Notice whether your right or left thumb is on top.

3. Unfold your hands.

4. Refold your hands with the other thumb on top.

Did you notice how you had to really think about doing it differently? It might have felt uncomfortable or even a bit *wrong*. That is the space of new learning. The awkwardness is simply an indication that you are in the territory of unknowing. Welcome the opportunity for growth this space provides. You can feel fearful or nervous about the new space, or excitedly welcome it as evidence of your personal growth. There's a saying that's often attributed to Einstein: "The definition of insanity is to do the same thing over and over again, and expect different results." Exercising your Inner Coach with new activities may feel awkward at first, because it is different for you. Once you move through the newness of it, your mind enjoys these new ways of being because you achieve the different results you want, and it easily becomes a habit.

* * *

Re-patterning is not about denying your (⇊) feelings or pretending that they don't exist. It's about helping you move through and process them with greater ease. Sometimes you just need to be heard, and you need to talk about or express your (⇊) feelings. Talking things through is an effective way of learning; however, you know the difference between when you're venting to work things through and when you're winding yourself into more of the (⇊) feeling. You've also been in the uncomfortable position of listening to a friend go on and on about something. You know it isn't productive, but what choice do you have?

Even though it was years ago, I remember the exact moment when I became consciously aware that my subconscious had moved me over the line all on its own, without the intervention of my conscious mind. I had experienced an extremely unpleasant argument and was really upset. I called a friend and began relating the story of the argument, digging myself further into the frustration and anger as I recalled and dramatized the details. My friend was listening, being sympathetic, and taking my side. Then I realized that although she was being supportive, I was actually feeling angrier. Rehashing the argument was in fact creating more anger within me, and I realized that my friend was starting to feel angry on my behalf.

Telling the story helped me feel better for a moment, but that fleeting feeling quickly disappeared, and I was rapidly feeling worse. The feel-better feelings were not growing; they were shrinking, and I was becoming a victim of the argument. I was letting it control my feelings, and I realized I didn't want to feel this way. My Inner Coach reminded me that I wasn't being supportive or caring of either my friend or myself!

In that split second my Inner Coach had stepped forward and begun to move my thoughts to the other side of the line, without me consciously moving them. I remember trying to hang on to the righteous indignation; after all, I was justified in my anger. My friend agreed! But even while I was feeding that anger with a recital of the wrongs I had been dealt during the argument, I could feel the anger slipping between my fingers. Those strong negative thoughts were being nudged aside by an even stronger voice.

My Inner Coach emerged: *Every moment I spend in anger is a moment lost forever to peace. Every minute of frustration could be a minute of harmony. Choose.*

The voice of the hurt victim within me threw back: *But he was wrong! It isn't what we agreed to! I was right!*

My Inner Coach replied, *I know. You're right, but how long do you choose to stay in the argument?*

With that thought, my Inner Coach had reengaged my reasoning mind. I didn't want to extend the time of the argument. It was nasty when it first happened, and here I was, a full hour later, feeding the argument and feeling worse. The argument may have begun with the other person, but I was responsible for giving it more power by retelling it.

We all have the power to choose our attitude in every moment and with every breath. Each action and thought and all our reactions and responses are our individual decisions. I was so excited that my Inner Coach had emerged when I wasn't consciously being vigilant of my thoughts. Right in the middle of a negative tailspin, my Inner Coach showed up and shifted my thoughts! I began to wonder where this wisdom had come from. Had I read it? Had I heard someone else say it?

As I was wondering where that clear, strong voice came from, I stopped. I realized it didn't *matter* where it came from; what was important was where it was taking me. The comment from my Inner Coach was putting me back on course. I had been unconsciously using my caring and compassionate friend to keep me in the frustration and anger. It wasn't intentional, but I realized that this is exactly what happens whenever we let each other rant and rave. We are reinforcing what we don't want and unknowingly creating more of the same. It feels supportive in the moment but, over time, is damaging.

Try This One! Practice:

SET TIME FRAMES

Sometimes, venting is exactly what you need, and a loving friend who listens as you blow off steam is a gift. Do yourself and your friends a favor by creating the habit of placing a time limit on the airing of grievances. This turns venting into an activity of *choice* instead of *chance*. I learned to do this with my students. I'd give them a couple of minutes on the clock to get it all out, and then we'd take a deep breath together and move into something more productive and positive.

Even when you're by yourself, you can exercise this conscious choice by setting the timer on your stove or phone, or plugging in the kettle when you feel the need to vent. Let out all the frustration, either verbally or in writing. When the kettle boils, stop speaking or put your pen down. You are done venting.

Giving yourself a short, specific time is a good way to release. Doing this for a friend can sometimes feel challenging, especially for women, whose upbringing involves listening empathetically to others' challenges. Being a good friend does involve listening, but it also means gently saying, "Enough; you are hurting yourself now."

As you become more observant of your own way of being, you'll begin to realize just how long you have carried some of those (⇓) stories and the resulting emotions. We've all known people who have harbored hurtful emotions for months, years, and decades, and witnessed the detrimental effect this has had on not only their outlook and perspective on life, but also their physical health. You, too, will have experienced an (⇓) emotion for some extended period. Even if you had every reason to feel that way, it doesn't serve you or anyone else to hang on to those energy-draining feelings. Every one of us is carrying emotions that do not support us and are injurious to our emotional and physical well-being. For you, it might be an old hurt that you're aware of, an emotion that erupts regularly, or a story you find yourself rehashing to a friend. You'll notice how thinking about it pulls your energy down.

Look back on the situation and pair of emotions you used in the "Re-patterning Statements for Conscious Decision," earlier in this chapter. Reinforce and personalize your re-patterning by adding a time frame. Have you experienced the (⇓) situation for a moment, an hour, a day, a week, a month, a year, or a lifetime? I've used *moment* in the following example. In the first instance, plug in the specific situation (S) you used in the Re-patterning Statements for Conscious Decision, and then the opposite of that situation (⇑ S):

Every moment I spend _____ (S) is a moment lost forever to _____ (⇑ S). I consciously choose to _____ (⇑ S).

Every moment I spend <u>arguing</u> is a moment lost forever to <u>working together</u>. I consciously choose to <u>work together</u>.

Now make the same statement again, but instead of the situations, use the emotions. Change the time frame to reflect your experience:

Every moment I spend in _____ (⇓) is a moment lost forever to _____ (⇑). I consciously choose _____ (⇑).

Every moment I spend in <u>rage</u> is a moment lost forever to <u>peace and harmony</u>. I consciously choose <u>peace and harmony</u>.

Whenever I use this style of Re-patterning Statement, with the built-in time frame, my Inner Critic says something like, *Well, if you put it that way . . .* It's a very persuasive way of framing the statement, so the mental shift literally becomes a no-brainer. I can feel the results of the productive conversation between my Inner Critic and my Inner Coach, and it changes my perspective. I'd encourage you to repeat this quick *time frame* exercise with all of the other pairs of emotions you've identified in the previous chapters. It sends an effective message to your subconscious.

What you think about you bring about; what you focus on expands. Your conscious decisions to focus that power in a positive direction will become habit for your powerful subconscious mind. Practicing Choice Statements provides your Inner Coach with something (⇑) that's at the ready to bring to your awareness. What emotions you feed flourish. What you think about manifests.

Many of us carry around toxic and negative emotions, just under the surface of our awareness. All it takes is some random argumentative words and our minds begin looking for other argumentative feelings. The current incident is blown out of proportion and connected and compared with every similar past unresolved hurt or unsupportive circumstance.

You've witnessed this in yourself and others. It's amazing how the subconscious connects present transgressions to previous ones so that you wind up in the victim place, where you experience everything from that perspective. With Choice Statements, your Inner Coach intervenes and uses that same amazingly powerful ability of your subconscious, but with your focus on connecting and contrasting the (⇓) and (⇑) feelings. Adding specific situations and time frames reinforces the choices you're making.

The Transition from Choice to Freedom

Think of your life as a painting. You choose the size, shape, and varieties of the paintbrushes you use, the parameters of your canvas, and the colors and designs that resonate for you! The beauty of life is that you create your own reality; however, this ability can result in frustration when your reality is not what you want. There's no need to blame yourself or beat yourself up for previous choices, whether conscious or unconscious. You can make a new one every moment. Learn what you can from the experience, and choose to move forward.

If you don't like where you are, change one thing. Small choices made consciously create large changes over time. Be aware of the choices you make. You are a product of the books you read, the music you listen to, and the people you associate with. All of this input shapes your decisions. Every moment is an opportunity for something new, different, or more supportive. Now that you understand how what you're feeling is transmitted out into your world, consciously *choose* your feelings, verbalize them, and watch with excitement and amazement as your dreams become your reality.

Many of my clients and students want to stop at the Choice stage because it feels good. It's a very mindful and empowering place; however, the next stage, Freedom, reinforces your Choice Statements by creating a clear vision of how your life will look when those conscious decisions are projected into the future.

❊　❊　❊　❊　❊

Chapter Seven

FREEDOM:
Trying It On

✳ ✳ ✳

"Twenty years from now, you will be more disappointed by the things that you didn't do than by the ones you did do. So throw off the bowlines. Sail away from the safe harbor. Catch the trade winds in your sails. Explore. Dream. Discover."

— ATTRIBUTED TO MARK TWAIN

The Freedom stage is the realm of your imagination projecting your choice into the future with excitement. Both the Freedom and Permission stages map out onto the future; the difference lies with which side of the line you are on. All of the tentativeness of Permission is left behind through the Choice you've made. Freedom is firmly on the supportive side, with your Inner Coach encouraging you. You feel yourself moving forward, knowing that the (⇑) feelings are real.

When learning the technique, some students are concerned that they are unsuccessful if their Inner Critic still shows up. If this happens to you, know that it's normal. As I've mentioned, beliefs come firmly tied to each other in groups; that is, they are always connected to other beliefs. If your Inner Critic does reappear, see it as an opportunity to re-pattern a larger piece of your belief system, and go back to the stage of Forgiveness or Permission, incorporating the new information into your statements.

We'll thoroughly explore how to work with your Inner Critic in Part III, "Positive Thoughts as Your Way of Being." For now, let's focus on understanding the Freedom stage more fully. Cast your mind back to a time when you were shopping for a new jacket. Remember trying on several different possibilities? Everything was too big, too small, not the right color or style, but then you found *the one!* Do you remember the feeling? You put on the jacket, and it felt right. You looked in the mirror from different angles, noticing how the shoulders fit perfectly as if you and the garment were one. The sleeves were the right length, and when you stretched your arms, there was room for you to move. You began thinking about how this jacket would fit with what you have, and when you would wear it. This is the feeling of the Freedom stage. You are creating the vision of your life with the (⇑) feelings, imagining and trying on ideas until you feel the *click* of "just right." Freedom is exhilarating and mind expanding, and reinforces the choice you've made to change your perspective.

Freedom is:

- Future oriented

- Visionary, with a realistic perspective

- Stepping firmly into the possibilities and seeing them as potential realities

- Using all of your senses to reinforce the supportive emotion

- Placing the new feeling into your life and seeing how it fits

- Beginning to redefine who you really are

- Knowing that things are right and perfect with this new awareness

Freedom is *not:*

- Pretending

- Getting bogged down in the specifics

- Irresponsible or foolhardy

You are ready for Freedom Statements when you are experiencing life in any of the following ways:

- Feeling excited about the choice you've made

- Feeling that something wonderful is about to happen

- Feeling awake and aware

- Imagining, visioning, or dreaming from a place of knowing

- Recognizing that the change is a done deal and that you're ready to move forward

- Experiencing certainty that what you want will manifest, even though you haven't yet achieved it

What Happens at the Freedom Stage?

You can feel your spirit rising and your eyes beginning to twinkle, and you're ready to take action. Propelled by your enthusiasm, you want to tell the world of your new realizations and discoveries! You are in the big-picture planning stages, not looking at the specific details but creating the vision. This is the beginning of the blueprint stage in which you've stepped out of the box where you'd resided and are thoroughly exploring the new reality for yourself.

Freedom is the stage of exclamation marks, options, and ideas. You project the (⇑) feelings into the future, knowing that they are becoming your reality. You're certain that you *are* doing things differently, and you want to share this with others. This is the childhood place of *Watch me do this!* You feel as if you've been let out of a cage, and you may realize that you held the key all along.

Your Inner Critic may come forward with an *It's about time* judgment, but your Inner Coach is strong, knows that everything is all right, and may reinforce that internal judgment with a Permission Statement like *I give myself permission to know that _____ (⇑) is happening in perfect time!* Freedom Statements let your body and mind know that you're no longer bound by your previous beliefs and are now moving forward, with the (⇑) emotion firmly anchoring the supportive thoughts into place. A new belief is being born. You're operating with a new playfulness and exuberance. You believe that it will all work out for the best, and that you can and will achieve what you desire. There's a smile on your face, your shoulders are back, and you are walking tall! Your energy is raised with the new and creative ideas that flood your awareness.

This is the stage of visioning mixed with action. Freedom Statements always include a verb after the word *free:* free to *create,* free to *experience,* free to *focus,* free to *explore,* and free to *learn.* Freedom begins connecting the new feeling to possible actions that build your future beliefs. This stage is where you gain confidence in bringing the (⇑) feeling to specific situations.

FREE TO BE YOUR BEST

Imagine: what if every decision you made in your relationships, work, and leisure time came from the supportive and strong place of your best self? Reflect for a moment on how your life will be different when your actions come from a place of abundance and joy rather than fear and lack. In your journal, list the (⇑) results you will achieve with this freedom. Capture how you will feel physically and emotionally. What are some recent decisions (D) you've made from this supportive place? Use some of the insights you gather to personalize the following statements. Be aware of the messages your body is bringing you through all of your senses, and add any new information to the statements.

RE-PATTERNING STATEMENTS
FOR JOY AND ABUNDANCE

I **forgive** myself for believing that I need to keep making decisions from fear and lack.

I give myself **permission** to make decisions from a place of joy and abundance.

Every decision made from a place of fear and lack is an opportunity lost. I consciously **choose** to make my decisions from joy and abundance from now on.

When I make my decisions from joy and abundance, I am **free** to create _____ (⇑).

I am **free** to create _____ (⇑) by making my decisions from the (⇑) side of the line.

A recent decision I've made from the place of abundance and joy is _____ (D), and it **felt** _____ (⇑). I **created** _____ (⇑) with this decision.

My strong and supportive decisions are created from joy and abundance, and it **feels** _____ (⇑).

The Learning Process at the Freedom Stage

Children's play is filled with boundless imagination and creativity. Kids have a thirst for knowledge, soaking up new words, ideas, skills, and abilities. It's as if they can't take it all in quite fast enough. The Freedom stage is that aspect of learning. The more you play with ideas and engage your creative imagination, the more supportive responses occur in your body. Your bloodstream is flooded with positive chemical concoctions, and your cell receptors move into a heightened state of receiving. As you reinforce your choices through Freedom Statements, your choices take on substance, and a new structure or plan emerges.

The similarity between the title of this chapter, "Freedom: Trying It On," and the Try This On! Practice activities in each chapter is intentional. The practices throughout the book reflect the experimental quality of the Freedom stage and strengthen your ability to incorporate the new learning into your daily way of being. All of this positive emotion is being registered, and your mind is reinforcing the new neural pathways. The new file folder in your subconscious is rapidly being filled with the latest experiences and connections you're making from this changed perspective. Your reticular activator is being firmly set to this new normal, and you're more aware of all that surrounds you that feeds into this place of creative thought.

The options are vast and real. This heightened state raises the vibration of your body, and you're transmitting a new message through your words, actions, and body language. You become a magnet for people, circumstances, and ideas at a similar vibration, which re-inforces your new way of being. You gain confidence in your ability to experience the (⇑) emotion you've been re-patterning toward, and you begin applying it to the situations at hand.

Try This On! Practice:

CREATE A VISION BOARD

Because of the playful nature of the Freedom stage, creating a vision board is a wonderful way to exercise your imagination. Finding pictures and words to express the feelings you want to increase in your life and placing them together on a piece of cardboard supports the resetting of your reticular activator. Adding to your vision board when you find things that elicit the feeling you truly want keeps your conscious mind aware of the changes. You can also tape the images onto a window or mirror and write the words with a dry-erase marker.

Focus your reticular activator on the vibration of what you desire by looking at your vision board first thing in the morning. At the end of the day, tell yourself a "good-night story" by going over the vision board. What happened today that moved you in that direction? Where in your body did you experience those feelings? Get yourself into that mode and then fall asleep in that open and creative energy, allowing your subconscious mind to soak up all your positive thoughts!

The Transition from Freedom to Affirmation

You are in the flow, and it shows. You're riding the wave of possibilities becoming reality, and you're fueled by your internal passions. This feeling is real, and you know it! You're stretching your previous limits and definitely enjoying the ride. You're imagining what you might do and how you might act from this strong place of being. You've spread your wings and are ready to take flight.

Just prior to takeoff, your Inner Coach is engaged to do a gear check. This is the next stage, Affirmation, where you look into your past experiences and connections to ensure that you're bringing what you need into your new way of being. Instead of embarking on this new adventure with fear, your Inner Coach is right there, reminding you that you have everything you need.

The Affirmation stage naturally follows the Freedom Stage, allowing you to move forward easily. Having been fueled by your passion and the excitement about where you're heading, your Inner Coach is ready and able to find the support you need to be confident in this new perspective!

※　※　※　※　※

Chapter Eight

AFFIRMATION:
Linking the New to the Known

✳ ✳ ✳

*"It takes courage to grow up and turn out to
be who you really are."*

— ATTRIBUTED TO E.E. CUMMINGS

As I mentioned in Chapter 3, the term *affirmation* is widely used in the personal-development field to refer to a statement that is repeated consistently over time with the intention of creating a new reality. In the context of Belief Re-patterning, though, *Affirmation* refers to a specific stage. All six stages of the process (*Forgiveness, Permission, Choice, Freedom, Affirmation,* and *Surrender*) use statements that are, by definition, affirmations, but the purpose of the ones at this fifth stage is unique. The word *affirm* means "to confirm or ratify the truth of something." *Affirmation,* then, is defined as "a statement that establishes something more firmly or provides evidence of a habit."

At the Affirmation stage, you're looking back into your past from new, solid grounding. Your Inner Coach is sorting through your memory for visible evidence to support your new perspective through *reinforcement, transferring,* and *modeling.* Let's look at each of these three methods to help you understand how you can use them in your personal re-patterning:

— **Reinforcement** is likely how you learned to add and subtract. Your teacher would give you a series of problems to solve that would provide the practice needed for you to learn. Rather than repeating *3 + 4 = 7* over and over and over again, students exhibit more effective learning when they apply the equation to different situations. Math problems like these reinforce learning: *There are 7 children; if 4 of them are boys, how many are girls? . . . You have 3 cars and 4 trucks; how many vehicles are there in total?* To build your own Affirmation Statements in Belief Re-patterning, you recall true, specific examples of when you experienced an (⇑) emotion. This helps you realize that although the circumstances may be new, you do have experience with the emotion and can reinforce that knowledge by applying it to the present situation.

— A second method for creating Belief Re-patterning affirmations is **transferring.** This involves recognizing how you interact with others and then transferring that to yourself. For example, if you're re-patterning toward an attribute such as patience, you might use a statement like *I am really patient with my granddaughter Casey. If I can be patient with her, I can learn to be patient with myself. I consciously practice being patient with myself until it becomes a new habit.*

— If your Inner Critic surfaces and insists that you've never felt the (⇑) feeling that you are re-patterning toward, look for examples of people you know who have that (⇑) quality. You've learned a lot by observing others and mimicking what they do. This mode of learning is called **modeling**, and it is useful and helpful as you create your own Affirmation Statements. Ask yourself, *Who do I know who exhibits this (⇑) trait in a way that I respect or admire?* Then create an Affirmation Statement using that individual's name and the trait, as in this example: *Camille is thoughtful. I'm learning to be thoughtful like she is.*

Inserting the idea of *learning, becoming,* or *practicing* into your statements usually overcomes any objections your Inner Critic may bring forth at this stage. Remember, the affirmations must feel completely true and real to be effective. This stage provides the reality check and has your Inner Coach gathering visible evidence that you can be successful in developing the new pattern. You're locking in the re-patterning using specific examples that will then trigger an additional subconscious reinforcement every time you see that person or do something similar. Once you've tapped into your memory with the first example, more examples will readily come to mind to support your learning.

Ten-year-old Adam and his siblings were removed from their mother's home by social services. This youngster had experienced significant abuse, both personally and through witnessing the abuse of the two younger children. Adam's foster-mother brought him to me to see if we could re-pattern whatever was causing his self-mutilating behavior and nightmares.

One of the words that arose during our re-patterning session was *peaceful*. Adam had no internal reference point for this word. He hadn't consciously experienced it in his abusive upbringing, nor had he been taught the feeling. Because he had no file folder in his subconscious for the concept, he hadn't even noticed peacefulness anywhere in his life experiences.

I used a series of Affirmation Statements with Adam to support him in creating this file folder: *I see and hear what it is like in Suze's backyard, and I learn about peacefulness in nature.* We walked outside and sat together on the grass. I asked him to close his eyes and experience the feeling of being in the backyard. When I asked him to describe the feeling, he said it felt quiet. Then I used a reinforcing affirmation, asking him to tell me when he'd experienced that good feeling of quiet before, and he told me that when his family was shopping and he was home alone, he liked the quiet. I asked him to repeat *When everything is quiet around me and inside of me, that is peaceful.*

I then helped Adam transfer this into his own way of being. I knew that he adored his younger sisters and was very good with them, so I added this affirmation: *I know how to help Maggie be peaceful so that she can go to sleep. I practice giving that same kind of peacefulness to myself. I am good at learning, and I'm practicing being peaceful.*

In order to further develop his understanding of the concept of *peaceful,* I asked Adam if he knew someone who seemed to have that peacefulness inside. He named one of his teachers, Mr. Blake, so we created a modeling affirmation containing that specific piece of information: *I am so grateful for Mr. Blake. He shows me what it's like to be peaceful inside. When I'm not sure how to be peaceful, I'll think of Mr. Blake and act the way I think he would act. I learn about being peaceful by watching and thinking about Mr. Blake.*

Adam's experience was extreme, but everyone, at times, has challenges with accessing specific supportive memories. When this occurs, look to nature or people whom you respect for examples. Reinforcing, transferring, and modeling allow you to link the new learning to what you already know, affirming its truth.

＊　　＊　　＊

The Affirmation Statements are not about convincing or pretending. They are designed to build on strengths that you already possess but may not have been aware of. The more you learn to reinforce your own accomplishments and attributes, the easier it will be for your Inner Coach to access specific examples in your experience. (In Part III, "Positive Thoughts as Your Way of Being," we'll focus on activities that will support your Inner Coach in doing so.)

Affirmation is:

• Looking to your past from a supportive perspective

• Focusing on visible evidence to reinforce the new pattern

- Positive self-reflection with specific, true examples

- Connecting the new to the known in your mind

- Real, not wishful, thinking

Affirmation is *not:*

- Stating or writing the same thing over and over again

- Trying to convince yourself that it is true

- Gradually wearing down old patterns and programming

You are ready for Affirmation Statements when you are experiencing life in any of the following ways:

- Anchoring your feelings with real examples

- Feeling reflective and supportive

- Looking for what you already know that applies to the new situation

- Identifying who might help you or support you in this new way of being

- Wondering how you will accomplish something and getting supportive answers from your Inner Coach

What Happens at the Affirmation Stage?

The Affirmation Statements reinforce your learning using specific memories. More than a decade ago, my friend Kathleen and I were chatting about a business venture we were building. I beat up on myself with the comment "My problem is that I am lousy at follow-up."

Kathleen's response was: "Help me understand how you can own your home and have two university degrees without being good at follow-up."

I am so grateful for her support of my Inner Coach that day. She gathered evidence that provided a new perspective for me. I realized that I did have great follow-up skills that I could transfer from other aspects of my life to my business through Affirmation Statements such as *I was really good at following up with my assignments in school. I am good at follow-up; that's how I got the mortgage and bought my own house. I now apply those follow-up skills to this new venture.*

The challenge I was experiencing was lack of confidence in a new endeavor. I used the skills that I knew I had developed in creating home ownership and educational success to build my self-confidence concerning my new business.

It's common for most of us to feel nervous or uncomfortable on entering a new situation, and we don't always have a friend there to remind us of our successes and abilities. Affirmation Statements help your Inner Coach leverage attributes and skills from one life area to another, fueling the supportive beliefs.

Quick Reflection:

BUILD YOUR CONFIDENCE

Think of a situation (S) where you would like more confidence. Jot it down in your journal, as well as how you currently feel about it. Are you disappointed in yourself, uncomfortable, nervous? Do you feel inadequate? Begin the practice of writing your (⇓) word with a single line drawn through it, with an arrow pointing to the opposite (⇑) word; for example, inadequate ⟶ confident. Doing this lets your mind know that the (⇓) feeling is being re-patterned into the (⇑) emotion.

The next series of Re-patterning Statements uses this pair of words to illustrate the different styles of creating Affirmation Statements and to support you in developing confidence in the situation (S) you just identified. To prepare for personalizing the statements, write three things in your journal:

• *Reinforcement:* A specific time, place, or set of circumstances in which you felt confident (1)

• *Transferring:* The name of someone whom you have supported in feeling confident (2)

• *Modeling:* The name of a specific person whose confidence you admire (3)

In the following statements, fill in the information beside the corresponding numbers.

RE-PATTERNING STATEMENTS
FOR INCREASING CONFIDENCE

I **forgive** myself for believing that I have to keep feeling
_____ (⇓) in/with _____ (S).

I give myself **permission** to focus on creating confidence
(⇑) in/with _____ (S).

I can feel _____ (⇓), or I can feel confident.
Since I can't feel both ways at the same time, I con-
sciously **choose** to create confidence and bring that to
_____ (S).

I am **free** to focus on creating confidence within me and
bring it to _____ (S).

I **know how it feels** to be confident; it happened when I
_____ (1).

I **know how to help others** feel confident; I supported
_____ (2) in feeling confident.

I **am grateful to** _____ (3) for showing me what
confidence looks like. When I'm not sure how to be confident in _____ (S), I'll think of what _____
(3) would do and try that.

I **am** feeling more confident, and I bring that increased
confidence to _____ (S).

By dipping into your memories and re-sorting them in light of a new perspective, you increase the intensity of the re-patterned feeling and strengthen the new neural pathway. This historical perspective provides a solid place of knowing, and you tap into that strength. Freedom Statements are about looking forward and visioning. Affirmation Statements involve looking back with the purpose of building the case for yourself that you already know a lot about this way of being, and you are applying that knowing to this new situation.

Learning is magnified through specific reinforcement. Recently I was encouraging my three-year-old granddaughter as she completed a puzzle. I said, "You are doing a great job!" Casey smiled and continued to randomly pick up pieces. Then I made the statement more specific: "Wow, Casey! Look how you figured out that the straight side with the blue stripe goes on the outside. That worked really well!" Casey immediately began looking for another straight-edged piece with a blue stripe.

I continued working with her. When I gave her general reinforcement, she smiled, but it didn't change her way of figuring out the puzzle. Every time I gave her specific feedback that accurately reflected what she had just done, it changed the way she approached the puzzle and sped up her ability to solve the problem. Your mind pays attention to specifics. Consciously giving yourself reinforcement with concrete examples re-patterns the way that you approach situations.

The Learning Process at the Affirmation Stage

I've had many conversations with people who say that affirmations don't work. Affirmations *always* work; it just depends on what you are affirming! If you're boldly stating something that you wish would come true but know isn't true now, your Inner Critic may call you on the lie. That affirms (⇓) feelings. Affirmation Statements in Belief Re-patterning always come from the truth of past experience, or the examples of others, reinforcing your Inner Coach and building belief in yourself. Every time you use them, you are strengthening the neural pathways in your brain and refining the focus of your reticular activator. Make certain your inner conversation and external declarations are in agreement.

If your Inner Coach discounts or disagrees with your Affirmation Statements, summon up a specific piece of evidence. For example, if your Inner Critic greets an Affirmation Statement like *I know how it feels to be abundant* with *No, you don't,* try again with a specific, true example: *I know how it feels to be abundant; it happened when I received a new-client referral from Dave last week.* If your Inner Critic persists, go back in the process to a Forgiveness or Permission Statement, using the specific information that was brought forth by your Inner Critic: *I forgive myself for believing that I am not abundant. I give myself permission to focus on the abundance that I experienced from Dave's referral, and expand it.* The steps do move logically from one stage to the next, but just as conversations move and flow, you can go back and forth among the steps according to feedback from your Inner Critic and Inner Coach.

The goal is to build supportive inner conversations that move you toward what you want to create, not just to repeat a series of statements. All of the examples throughout this book have been in a script format. Many of my students and clients initially want to memorize statements. The goal is to train your mind to work through the six stages using specific examples in your life, personalizing the statements. The scripts are like training wheels, guiding you until you achieve your own balance and comfort with the technique. You will begin moving through each of the six stages with ease. The Affirmation stage is where you have been personalizing the Belief Re-patterning process since Chapter 1 by inserting specific examples from your life experience. Transfer your ability to personalize the Affirmation Statements to the other five types of Re-patterning Statements.

Some people believe they need to repeat Affirmation Statements over and over for several days or weeks. In Chapter 2 you experienced how repeating exactly the same thing over and over can create doubt in your mind and actually block learning. I gave you the example of your partner or child coming up to you and saying, "I love you," three times in a row. But when the same feeling is expressed in three different ways—first, "I love you," and then a minute later, "I love how you smile when I say that!" and finally, "I love that you are a part of my world!"—you experience an expanded feeling of love.

Learning is most effective whenever you achieve this expansive place of applying the new feeling or concept to other situations. In the process of re-patterning, whenever you're completing a focused series of Re-patterning Statements, change the examples and be as specific as you can. Afterward it is extremely effective to reinforce the re-patterning over the next few days by focusing your attention on creating the (⇑) feeling in different situations.

There is a big difference between repetition and reinforcement. All learning needs reinforcement, not repetition. For this reason, I suggest to my clients and students that they simply write down the (⇑) word. You can write this word on a card that you carry with you, or highlight it in your journal. By writing down just the (⇑) feeling that you are re-patterning, you free your mind to integrate it in many different ways and embed it into various situations. This reinforces the emotion and expands the feeling. Rather than repeating the exact Affirmation Statement over and over again, thereby creating doubt, you're actually strengthening the new learning through reinforcement and application to different situations.

A classic classroom-management technique is to catch students doing something right and then reinforce it. Reinforcing positive behavior is far more effective than punishing poor behavior. This works with children and animals, yet when it comes to ourselves, we often punish instead of praise. What if you began noticing and reinforcing your own good behavior?

The *That's not like me* exercise I explained in Chapter 4 quickly evolves into another statement, one that consciously acknowledges and celebrates the supportive behavior and habits you had been taking for granted: *That's just like me!*

Try This One! Practice:

"THAT'S JUST LIKE ME!"

That's just like me! is an easy way to give yourself a pat on the back. Use this reinforcing statement whenever you want to experience more of a (⇑) feeling; for example, *That's just like me to be joyful!* Or to celebrate an accomplishment, use *That's just like me to have an organized desk!* The more you use this phrase, the stronger your Inner Coach becomes. *That's just like me!* re-patterns the way you define your true self through noticing and then consciously reinforcing your positive attributes and behaviors.

The Transition from Affirmation to Surrender

Studies have shown that children hear "no" many more times a day than "yes." This happened to all of us, reinforcing our reticular activator to focus on what was wrong rather than what was right. When I was a child, I remember being frustrated when adults would notice the one thing that I did incorrectly. I felt that they didn't even notice all of the day-to-day things that I successfully completed. This is a common experience. It's no wonder that when we grow up, we continue to focus on the 5 percent that we have yet to accomplish instead of the 95 percent that we have done. We look at the hole instead of the doughnut. It's time to change that habit!

Most of us are really good at gathering evidence to support the hole.

By choosing to focus your energy on gathering positive evidence and support through the use of Affirmation Statements, you will refocus your reticular activator on what is right, good, and positive in your world. That will shift the pattern you developed in childhood. By celebrating your accomplishments and acknowledging your strengths, you support your Inner Coach.

Affirmation of the qualities you wish to possess can be reinforced consciously and subconsciously, and when you use your mind in both ways, the learning becomes solid! You're linking new information, situations, and emotions with supportive memories, and through modeling and transferring, you reinforce a new way of being. As you consciously affirm your prior knowledge and connect it to where you are now, you begin to really define who you are and who you are becoming. The Surrender stage is where you claim this new way as *your* way.

✻　✻　✻　✻　✻

Chapter Nine

SURRENDER:
"Who I Really Am"

✳   ✳   ✳

"Surrender means accepting this moment, this body, and this life with open arms. Surrender involves getting out of our own way and living in accord with a higher will, expressed as the wisdom of our own heart. Far more than passive acceptance, surrender uses every challenge as a means of spiritual growth and expanded awareness."

— DAN MILLMAN

When my kids were small, we camped regularly at a wonderful spot on the shores of Lake Windermere in British Columbia. Shadybrook was a haven for families. Everyone looked out for each other, and the kids experienced the freedom of summer with few limitations. There was one rite of passage that was important: the middle-of-the-lake test. Once they passed this test, the kids were allowed to play in the lake without a parent present. Until they had accomplished this, they could go to the beach but needed to wait for one of the adults before going in the water.

I remember the year that my daughter Charis achieved her goal. She started talking about it in the spring: "This year, I'm doing it!" Summer finally arrived, and the three-hour drive to the campground was filled with her excitement. *This* summer she would get to go swimming with the big kids.

We arrived at Shadybrook and piled into the Zodiac boat. Her dad navigated us to the middle of the lake and turned off the motor. I dove in. All was quiet, in anticipation of Charis's moment. The middle-of-the-lake test involved jumping in and treading water with me for three minutes. She sat in the boat, held back by fear. Her Inner Critic was taking her out of the game. I continued to tread water, waiting for her to literally step over the line and jump in. Back and forth went her resolve. After 15 minutes, I climbed back into the boat. Charis was upset. I hugged her and let her know that when she was ready, she would just do it. The time wasn't right. We headed back to shore.

The next morning Charis awoke with steely commitment in her eyes and a fire in her belly. She could hardly wait. We all piled back into the boat. Her dad picked the spot and turned off the motor. I dove in and had barely surfaced when Charis took the leap. With arms stretched wide and a big smile on her face, she confidently jumped. She bobbed to the surface and began treading water easily. What had terrified her yesterday was easy today. She had surrendered to her new way of being in perfect time. By the end of the day, she was jumping in and out of the boat as if she had been doing it forever. It had become her new normal.

* * *

The Surrender stage is about accepting a new truth for yourself. It's the declaration: *This is the way I create my world! This is who I really am!* No longer wondering what to do, you trust your knowing and act with integrity. Your beliefs are in alignment with your being, and you've reset your perspective concerning who you really are. Rather than being driven by your unmet needs, you are propelled forward by your values. What you once perceived as deficits or weaknesses, you now recognize as opportunities to develop new strengths. You know you can and will re-pattern anything you choose.

Most people associate *surrendering* with handing something over or giving up their rights. Think of this stage as giving up the old pattern that no longer serves you and relinquishing its control over you. At some point in the past, you surrendered to the beliefs that are now in your way. You gave your power to a way of perceiving and being that may have supported you then but no longer works. Through the re-patterning process, you are consciously surrendering to an emotional state of being that supports you in the present moment.

A deeper look into the actual meaning of the word *surrender* takes us to the essence of this stage. According to the *Concise Oxford English Dictionary, surrender* also means to ". . . cease from resistance . . . give oneself over to habit, emotion, influence." It is this dual action of surrender—the dismissing of the old, combined with giving yourself over to a new way of being—that is the power of this stage. Remember, the decisions are all yours throughout the re-patterning process. You are creating the emotional energy that guides your decisions. You are surrendering to your true self.

I love supporting individuals in uncovering their true selves and stepping courageously into living from a place of alignment. I am committed to living authentically and to building Belief Re-patterning in alignment with universal laws. When I developed the initial course offerings, the focus was on clearing obstacles and moving through challenges. As I observed those clients who were studying Belief Re-patterning, it became crystal clear to me that Surrender was not the end of a six-stage *clearing* process, but rather the beginning of a new way of being.

This place of acceptance my students were achieving through regular re-patterning was allowing the creation of so much more in each of their lives. They were discovering for themselves that the technique not only got rid of the blocks they were experiencing, but also opened doors to places that they had thought were inaccessible. The act of surrendering was creating new opportunities for them that had not seemed to be available when their focus was on getting *unstuck*.

Whatever we focus on expands, and Belief Re-patterning focuses on the creation of alignment: body, mind, and soul. If your focus is on *clearing* blocks, the Law of Attraction will bring you more blocks to clear.

Belief Re-patterning really works well to get you back on track when things are out of sync, but proactively integrating the technique into your day-to-day life is even more powerful. Surrender to a supportive way of living, rather than wait for something to be wrong and then fix it. Focusing on creating means more creating. Focusing on clearing means more clearing, which was not what anyone ever wanted. Of course, we all want the pain to go away, but what each of us *really* wants is a purposeful, joyful, and loving life. The underlying intention of Belief Re-patterning is creation. It helps you to consciously create what you want rather than focus on *fixing* what you perceive to be *wrong* in your life. As you create an authentic way of being, life flows.

When you uncover your true essence and then explore what you can do from that place, you achieve amazing things! You are compelling when you act from the authenticity that Surrender clicks into place. You are working with the Law of Attraction. All of the energy that was once wrapped up in the old worry and doubt is now available to you for creating what you truly desire with positive and supportive beliefs.

Surrender is:

- A very present and solid belief in yourself

- Embracing and claiming who you are

- Living your vision and putting the re-patterning into action

- Recognizing that you are worthy regardless of circumstances, events, or the opinions of others

- Understanding and truly accepting yourself

- Finding your security within

Surrender is *not:*

- Giving up anything except an old way that no longer serves you

- Compromising on your ideals and values

You are ready for Surrender Statements when you are experiencing life in any of the following ways:

- Feeling comfortable with who you are and who you are becoming

- Feeling that everything is operating in your favor (because it *is!*)

- Trusting in yourself and your ability to meet whatever happens

- Being the human being that is right for you

- Feeling confident of your worth

- Focusing on what is working

- Encouraging yourself and really listening to your inner voices

- Loving yourself

What Happens at the Surrender Stage?

You recognize that your beliefs can and do change rapidly. You operate with a deep knowing and respect for yourself. People are drawn to you because you've learned to appreciate and value yourself.

Your Inner Coach is the predominant voice, and you welcome the insights of your Inner Critic. No longer ignoring or pushing aside these disparaging comments or accepting them as truth, you recognize that the messages of your Inner Critic are there to point you in the direction of your dreams by letting you know what is in the way. Now that you are listening, these messages are delivered in a kinder and gentler way.

The Learning Process at the Surrender Stage

You've sorted through the chaos and come to a place of inner balance and acceptance. You are aware of the learning process and welcome the changing of your beliefs, because you've experienced the vitality and energy that come from the alignment of your body, mind, and soul.

You begin the process consciously by repeating the Re-patterning Statements, and then your wonderful subconscious mind begins to run the patterns. Because the (⇑) feeling is more pleasurable and your physical body enjoys the chemical compound created by that feeling, you go there quite naturally. For a while you have two pathways, the old one and the new one. The more frequently the (⇑) new one is consciously practiced, the more rapidly it becomes habit. The (⇓) old pathway remains, but you will use it less and less often.

In high-stress moments, when you switch to fight-or-flight mode, the (⇓) old pathway may be the one that your subconscious uses. Be gentle with yourself if this happens. It doesn't mean that you aren't successful; it's just that at these times, old habits can kick in again. When this occurs, consciously move your focus to (⇑) supportive feelings and strengthen them with additional Freedom, Affirmation, and Surrender Statements. This will deepen the neural-pathway connections and put you back on the track that supports you.

Think back to the elementary school you attended. Remember the big playing field that surrounded it? There was always a pathway worn from the far corner across the field to the school door. If you grew up in a colder climate, you remember the first deep snowfall of winter. It covered up the path, and the kids trudged through the newly fallen snow, making a fresh path. Over the winter, this new path became the usual path. With the warmer spring weather, the snow melted, revealing two paths: the old one from last year and the new one. Everyone began using the shortest and most direct route. The other path would ultimately grow over from disuse, only showing up as a puddle after a big rainstorm. Over time, even this reminder of the old path would disappear, covered over with grass.

The process of creating new neural pathways in your mind is similar. Your subconscious mind always uses the shortest and most direct path it can find. In the beginning you will be aware of your conscious choice to be in the (⇑) feelings. As you put into action the vision you created at the Freedom stage and reinforce it through Affirmation Statements, you will naturally Surrender to the supportive way of being. Consciously choosing the supportive path in times of stress trains your subconscious to use the (⇑) path. The old, unsupportive neural pathway will no longer be accessed by your subconscious and will, in essence, disappear from lack of use. Your thoughts, actions, and beliefs have clicked into place. Your body, mind, and soul are aligned. Congratulations! You've created a new, supportive belief.

Quick Reflection:

SURRENDER TO YOUR BEST SELF

Many people focus on their shortcomings or the places where they are challenged (⇓), and define themselves that way. Through re-patterning, you're focusing on your strengths and attributes. It's a new habit, and with practice you will become more comfortable with surrendering to who you really are, as illustrated by your strengths. Since what you focus on expands, surrendering to your strengths will expand them. It makes sense to concentrate on (⇑) characteristics, and all of the re-patterning exercises, including the Re-patterning Statements, strengthen your Inner Coach.

If you're having some challenges in focusing on your (⇑) attributes, think of individuals in your life who recognize your strengths. Until now you may have deflected their compliments. A healthy self-concept doesn't rely on the perceptions of others, but it makes sense to look to those who value you and learn from their perceptions. Positive influences in your life such as coaches, teachers, parents, and friends have given you compliments based on their observations. Have you let their praise sink in and contribute to your healthy self-concept, or have you been in the unconscious habit of brushing their observations aside?

Identify some of the positive influences in your life and list their first names in your journal, leaving a line or two between each name. What would they tell me that they appreciate or admire about you? Reflect on and jot down the strengths you think they see in you.

You can use these names and the strengths these people see in you to personalize your Re-patterning Statements. Practice claiming your attributes and support your Inner Coach by writing out the following statements in your journal using the specific names (N) and strengths (S) you've identified, and then reinforce the attributes by saying the statements aloud. I've given you two real examples of positive influences in my life. Kathleen and Phil are great, longtime friends of mine who have unknowingly supported my Inner Coach.

I am so grateful to _____ (N); he/she sees my _____ (S) and _____ (S).

I am so grateful to Kathleen; she sees my potential and creativity.

I am so grateful to _____ (N); he/she believes in my _____ (S).

I am so grateful to Phil; he believes in my ability to succeed.

I appreciate _____ (N) for helping me claim my _____ (S).

I thank _____ (N) for helping me recognize my _____ (S).

I value _____ (N) for encouraging me by saying I have _____ (S).

Gratitude: Turn It Inward

The power of gratitude has been well documented, and you understand the importance of expressing gratitude to others and to your higher power. Have you thought about giving gratitude to yourself? It is an extremely effective way of surrendering to a supportive way of being.

Whenever we thank others, it raises both their vibration and ours. It feels good. Gratitude creates a chemical mixture in our bodies that feeds our receptor cells in a positive way. Combining gratitude with any other (⇑) feeling deepens the corresponding neural pathway significantly.

Turning your thanks toward yourself is a powerful practice, because it also exercises your ability to receive compliments from others. When we downplay these remarks, we not only belittle ourselves, but also unintentionally disregard the giver of the compliment. Practicing self-gratitude will open you to receiving admiration and gratitude from others with greater ease.

When in doubt, give gratitude to yourself for what you know. When you're sad, offer appreciation for the times you've experienced joy. When you're lonely, thank yourself for the connections you've made. Acknowledge yourself for being the best *you* that you can be at any given moment. Gratitude is the shortcut to surrender, and will always intensify the effectiveness of re-patterning.

In the next re-patterning series, notice the physical changes you experience when you add self-gratitude to each type of statement. Read each one, and feel into your body's response. Then say the same statement again, adding the suggested expression of gratitude. Inhale and exhale again. You will likely notice that you breathe more deeply when you add gratitude to your statements and that the (⇑) feelings intensify.

RE-PATTERNING STATEMENTS FOR SELF-GRATITUDE

I **forgive** myself for all the times that I deflected a compliment in the past. I **forgive** myself for believing that I wasn't good, worthy, or deserving enough. It was not my intention to hurt the other person or myself . . .

. . . and I am **grateful** to myself for learning how to receive compliments.

I give myself **permission** to really hear compliments from others and let them sink in from now on . . .

. . . and I **thank** myself for being open to hearing compliments.

I can deflect compliments, or I can receive them. I consciously **choose** to receive them and let them in . . .

. . . and I **thank** myself for recognizing that I am worthy and deserving.

I'm **free** to receive compliments from others and accept them with ease . . .

. . . and I am **thankful** that I can acknowledge my own successes and strengths.

I **know** how it feels to give compliments to others, and I give these good feelings to myself . . .

. . . and I am **grateful** to my Inner Coach for this support.

I **am** consciously practicing receiving compliments from others with ease . . .

. . . and I **appreciate** and value *me!*

Self-gratitude moves you through the six stages more quickly, and is an extremely helpful way to engage your Inner Coach in dealing with any objections that may surface from your Inner Critic.

Imagine that you are re-patterning toward being in balance. You might use a Surrender Statement like *I am in balance—body, mind, and soul.* Your Inner Critic might jump in with a comment such as *You weren't in balance this weekend when you stayed up late!* Your Inner Coach could reply with a combination Forgiveness and Gratitude statement like, *I **forgive** myself for not getting enough sleep Saturday night, and I am so **grateful** to myself for going to bed early Sunday night.* Learning to incorporate self-gratitude in your inner conversations is a wonderful gift to give to yourself.

Picture inviting friends over for a meal. They come in and sit down, you serve the fabulous dishes that you've planned and prepared, and everyone eats. At the end of the meal, they get up from the table and go out the door. No one acknowledges or celebrates the event in any way. Nothing is said about the dinner or your efforts. They just leave, chattering about their next activity. You probably wouldn't feel motivated to invite this group over again. It would be challenging to build up your energy another time.

I hope this scenario never happens to you, but you can imagine how you would feel if it did. Yet these same feelings are what you unknowingly create within yourself when you finish one thing and jump immediately to the next without acknowledging and celebrating the completion.

How often have you really focused on a project or task, completed it, and then moved directly on to the next thing with no acknowledgment, no celebration? You've unconsciously created the same feelings as those hypothetical friends. You're keeping yourself on that old treadmill, believing that if you just get this one more thing done, you will stop, even though you know that one more thing leads to one more thing and just one more *little* thing, until you feel tired and overwhelmed. You also know that if someone comes in and makes a positive comment about what you're doing, it boosts your energy and productivity.

Unfortunately, there isn't always someone else there to give you the acknowledgment you need, so encouraging yourself with self-gratitude allows you to fulfill your own needs. Motivational encouragement from others works for a short time, but for sustained growth and change, self-encouragement from a place of authentic surrender is key.

Try This One! Practice:

GIVE YOURSELF MOMENTS OF SELF-GRATITUDE

Self-gratitude isn't the same as being boastful, and you won't become egotistical. Both of those characteristics come from the (⇓) side of the line. You're speaking from the (⇑) side with the voice of your Inner Coach. I use my favorite self-gratitude exercise whenever I need a boost. I like doing it, because it simply makes use of time that otherwise would be wasted!

When I'm driving and come to a red light, I give myself gratitude out loud until the light turns green. I'll say things like, "I'm grateful for my car and that I always make my payments on time," or "I am thankful for my great eyesight and for my safe driving record." My comments don't need to be about driving. They can be reflections on the good I've experienced that day: "I'm thankful for the love I feel for my daughter who just called," or "I'm thankful for the lifestyle I've created that makes it possible to enjoy flexibility and freedom every day." When the light turns green, I move forward with a smile on my face and a stronger Inner Coach! Try this exercise today. If you're driving with children, this is a great family game.

Another easy way to increase your self-gratitude is to tie it to thanking others. Develop the habit of silently thanking yourself whenever you thank someone else. Here are some examples of what your Inner Coach might silently say to you whenever you express your gratitude to others. A potential inner conversation is in italics after the outward expression:

- "Thank you for inviting me to lunch." *And thank you to me for developing such a wonderful friendship.*

- "Thank you for fixing my car." *I am so grateful that I have the income to pay for the repairs!*

- "I really appreciate your picking me up." *I'm so grateful that I asked for the help I needed.*

Thanking yourself for specific things several times a day increases the positive energy in your body and sends it rippling into your life. If you didn't express your appreciation to others, you would find that they wouldn't be particularly motivated to continue to support you. Yet, most people charge forward, never stopping to thank themselves or acknowledge what they've accomplished, focusing only on what is yet to be done. Giving conscious, regular gratitude to yourself builds the strength of your Inner Coach. Self-gratitude is a way of recognizing that you are deserving and worthy of good in your life.

Gratitude is an excellent way of reinforcing the Surrender stage. When you don't know what to say, do, or be, give gratitude to others, your higher power, and yourself. It will always bring you to surrendering to who you really are.

Surrender to your positive attributes. By making changes in the input you receive whenever possible, you strengthen your Inner Coach's ability to support you when you need it. Thank yourself for who you really are and the uniqueness you bring to the world.

From Forgiveness to Surrender

I often liken learning the Belief Re-patterning process to learning to drive a car with a standard transmission. Moving through the six stages is like shifting gears. While you're learning to re-pattern, there can be a bit of a lurch between the stages, just as when you're discovering how to use a clutch. With practice, you can effortlessly shift gears. Similarly, the Try This On! Practices and Quick Reflections in each chapter have given you practical experiences in re-patterning, and you're beginning to navigate the process with greater understanding and ease.

You move from feelings of being stuck by engaging your personal internal engine. The fuel for your engine is your passion, which flows more rapidly as you re-pattern. In a car, if you push the gas pedal to the floor without engaging the gears, you flood the engine and stall out. Similarly, your passion can overwhelm you and stall out if you don't engage in a step-by-step process to move yourself forward. The gears in this metaphor are the six stages, and gratitude oils those gears.

The stage of Forgiveness is first gear. As you shift up to Permission, you feel your personal power kicking in, and at Choice you are comfortably cruising along at a low speed. With Freedom and Affirmation, you get your internal revs up, just like fourth and fifth gear. Surrender is sixth gear, and your engine operates effortlessly, cruising along effectively and efficiently.

The additional practice activities in Part III will support you by further integrating your learning of Belief Re-patterning into a way of being. The Re-patterning Statements will flow, and you will find yourself shifting your energy up with greater ease.

You are the only one who defines you. When you surrender to being who you *really* are, you are your authentic self; you are in the flow of life. You'll find yourself experiencing ease where you used to struggle, peace where frustration used to enter, and acceptance of yourself where anger once ruled.

Each of us is unique, and using Belief Re-patterning to strengthen your supportive self-perceptions extends to how you experience life. The way you are in the world is reflected back to you by the people you meet and the interactions you have every day. If what is reflected back feels good to you, you are being your true self. Whenever you experience resistance, there is an opportunity to grow and learn.

My attention is drawn to a postcard I purchased on a trip to the National Civil Rights Museum in Memphis. It sits in a frame on top of my bookcase and features a picture of Martin Luther King standing at his desk with a portrait of Gandhi on the wall over his shoulder. The postcard is titled "Integrity. Dr. Martin Luther King, Jr." and includes this quote: "When your character is built on spiritual and moral foundation, your contagious way of life will influence millions." It is a touchstone, reminding me daily to be who I really am and to act from that place of integrity.

As I watch my clients and students step into being their true selves, I observe them realizing their dreams. Through using the six stages of Belief Re-patterning—*Forgiveness, Permission, Choice, Freedom, Affirmation,* and *Surrender*—you flip the switch to positive thoughts and build your own solid foundation. Energy radiates from this solid, centered place of knowing who you really are. You've consciously created a more supportive core of beliefs about who you are and the way life works. Since your beliefs translate into your words and actions, this changes the way you are in the world.

In the following chapters, you'll discover more practical ways to integrate these six stages into your daily experiences to create your own *contagious way of life.*

❋　❋　❋　❋　❋

Part III

✳ ✳ ✳

POSITIVE THOUGHTS AS YOUR WAY OF BEING

Chapter Ten

CROSSING THE LINE WITH EASE

✳ ✳ ✳

"Energy goes where attention flows."

— ALAN COHEN

One of the things I remember hearing when I was a child was, "You're crossing the line!" You may have heard that warning as well. It was a clear signal from adults that continuing in the direction I was going wouldn't turn out well. If I kept up the behavior, I wasn't going to like the consequences. As an adult I've defined my own line: it's the one between love and fear, between light and darkness, and between supportive and unsupportive. Sometimes the line is blurry, or difficult for me to see, but the more I listen to my Inner Coach and Inner Critic, the more clarity I experience.

I use the concept of *crossing the line* to guide me to what I want to create. I can feel when I cross over into unsupportive emotions, thoughts, or behaviors. I've changed my perspective on this. Rather than use the line as a precursor to punishment, I use it as a place of neutrality, a place of decision making. The line in Belief

Re-patterning is the Choice stage. Rather than see it as something to be avoided, as I did when I was a child, I've re-patterned the image of *crossing the line* into something that my Inner Coach uses. It's like a speed bump on the continuum of my emotions: on one side of the line is everything that drags my energy down; on the other is everything that supports me. The line itself is neutral, giving me a grounded perspective in the present moment, where I decide whether I want to go (⇓) or (⇑) from the line. And when I frame it that way, the choice is obvious!

Our world operates in contrasts and opposites. We often define something as what it is *not,* rather than what it *is.* It's a natural way of learning. The popular children's program *Sesame Street* has a regular segment called "One of These Things Is Not Like the Others" that helps children learn to sort and categorize. Young kids are taught to look for what's out of place and to focus on what doesn't fit. These learning activities train children's minds to look for differences, building neural pathways by connecting one thing to another.

We learn through identifying contrasts and making connections. Ask people what they want, and the usual response is either a blank stare or an explanation of what they don't want. You can use this natural way of connecting opposites to re-pattern your neural pathways to focus on what is right and would fit, instead of what's wrong and doesn't fit.

Both what you want and don't want are registered in your body with emotion. When a person says, "I don't want to work here anymore," the emotion that is registered is, *I don't like the way I feel in this job.* The employee may want to feel less bored or less taken for granted. If there were a way to feel more stimulated or appreciated without quitting, *that's* what the person would want. Similarly, saying, "My job is great!" translates as *I like the way I feel in this job!*

Moving Yourself to the Line

Rarely do we want material things. What we really want are the feelings we think we will have when we get the material things. Your emotional response to anything or anyone in any situation reinforces what you want and don't want. If something feels good now and feels good later, you are on the supportive side of the line. If it feels good now and bad later, you are on the unsupportive side of the line.

When I become aware that I am on the (⇊) side of the line, my only focus is to get myself to the line itself. Trying to move from an (⇊) emotional state to an (⇑) emotional state can feel like too big a leap. Identifying the (⇑) emotional state is useful in getting you to the line, but trying to talk yourself into feeling up when you aren't is counterproductive. Knowing where you're headed and getting yourself to the line is workable.

Imagine someone who has fallen into the ocean and is in danger of drowning—which an (⇊) emotional state can often feel like. The first thought is usually one of panic, releasing adrenaline and providing a burst of energy. Staying in a state of panic won't help the person get to shore. Focusing on the opposite of panic, like the feeling of safety or security, is helpful. Knowing what feelings to move toward will focus all of the person's energy on getting to shore.

Similarly, when you find yourself in a downward spiral, think of what the opposite, positive space is. That will help you get to the line. Forgiveness and Permission Statements get you to the line, the Choice stage. You are present and weighing the two options. Continuing with the metaphor of falling into the ocean, the Choice stage is where your feet touch the sand and you climb onto the shore. At that point, moving into what you really want is much easier: go back and drown in the (⇓) feelings, or move forward into the (⇑) feeling that you really want.

A couple of years ago, I resolved to make all my decisions from the (⇑) side of the line from that moment on. What a profound effect that simple resolution has had on everything in my life! When I feel frustrated, angry, tired, or any other emotion that pulls my energy down, my *only* decision is to get myself to the line. I know that any decision I make when I feel (⇓) will not be productive. I identify the supportive opposite of that (⇓) feeling and then consciously create the (⇑) feeling. That gets me to a place where I can consciously choose between the two.

Do you notice that I am deciding which emotion I want to feel rather than what course of action to take? Once I am at the line, the place of choice, everything becomes clearer. I know what I want to feel more of, and I am able to make more productive and effective decisions that lead to the actions that will create more of the (⇑) feeling. Using the concept of the line allows you to consciously spend more time on the side of it that supports you. We naturally gravitate toward what makes us feel good.

Quick Reflection:

ACTIVITIES, EMOTIONS, AND OPPOSITES

In this Quick Reflection you'll develop a visual representation in your journal of the process you've learned to go through to prepare for the Re-patterning Statements. You'll need about ten minutes for this one and it's an important step in clarifying what you've learned, so I encourage you to find the time. The conscious practice of sorting daily events and experiences to one side of the line or the other strengthens those neural pathways. Just like flexing your physical muscles, this process exercises your mind to automatically move into what you do want to feel.

In your journal, draw a line down the middle of a page and set up a chart like the following one. Then reflect on the past day or two, and sort the events, activities, and situations you experienced. Did they drain your energy or lift it? Write each situation on the applicable side of the line using a separate line for each situation.

Drains My Energy (⇓) | **Lifts My Energy (⇑)**

Arguing about money

Reading with Jacob

In re-patterning, the situation is just a situation. Rather than trying to resolve it, you use it to determine the feeling you want to experience. Acknowledge and write the (⇓) feeling that drains your energy in each situation. In my example, the feeling is frustration. Remember to put a line through the (⇓) words pointing to the (⇑) opposites you've identified on the other side—*peace,* in my example. Identifying your (⇑) feeling before you begin to re-pattern gives your mind the impetus to let go of the (⇓) feeling and move you to the line. Acknowledging the (⇑) activities and the emotions they create—*connected,* in my example— anchors your Inner Coach while you examine the emotions that drain your energy.

Drains My Energy (⇓)   **Lifts My Energy (⇑)**

Arguing about money   ~~frustration~~ → peace

                                        connected
                                        Reading with Jacob

Next, write down a recent situation in which you experienced the (⇑) feeling. It does not need to relate in any way to the energy-draining situation.

Drains My Energy (⇓)   **Lifts My Energy (⇑)**

Arguing about money   ~~frustration~~ → peace

                                        Being in
                                        the mountains

The interesting thing about creating a chart like this is that once you have done this consciously with several past situations, you will discover that your subconscious will start this process for you as you ex- perience current situations. Fill in this basic series of statements with each set of specific emotions and ex- amples you brought *over the line.* Say them out loud as you write them in your journal.

RE-PATTERNING STATEMENTS
FOR MOVING ACROSS THE LINE

I **forgive** myself for believing that I need to keep feeling
_____ (⇓).

I forgive myself for believing that I need to keep feeling
frustrated.

I give myself **permission** to be _____ (⇑).

I give myself permission to be peaceful.

I can be _____ (⇓), or I can be _____ (⇑); I
choose to be _____ (⇑).

I can be frustrated, or I can be peaceful; I choose to be
peaceful.

I am **free** to increase _____ (⇑) in all areas of my
life.

I am free to increase peacefulness in all areas of my life.

I **know** how it feels to be _____ (⇑). I **felt**
_____ (⇑) when I _____ [recent situation].

I know how it feels to be peaceful. I felt peaceful when I
was in the mountains.

I **am** _____ (⇑).

I am peaceful.

Because the (⇑) side of the chart creates positive emotion, your reticular activator is triggered. Using this (⇑) information to create future Re-patterning Statements provides further reinforcement of the neural pathways.

Try This On! Practice:

DO WHAT HELPS YOU CROSS THE LINE

Notice that in the previous reflection you didn't focus any time or energy on trying to figure out what to do about the situation. You simply identified the (⇓) feeling, removed it from the (⇓) situation, and then used it to name the opposite. Then you re-patterned toward the (⇑) feeling, associating it with an unrelated (⇑) event. From this place of strength on the side of the line that supports you, you can then look back at the unsupportive situation and ask yourself this question:

What one thing could I do right now that would increase my feeling of _____ (⇑) when I think about _____ [(⇓) situation]?

What one thing could I do right now that would increase my feeling of _peacefulness_ when I think about _money_?

Listen for your Inner Coach to direct you toward what action you can take to connect the (⇑) feeling with the energy-draining situation. My Inner Coach suggested that I file my receipts, so while I do so, I focus my mind on situations in which I feel, and have felt, peaceful. This reinforces the (⇑) feeling and makes the mental connection between it and the ⇓ situation.

> **Set your intention for the activity out loud:**
>
> I am _____ (⇑), and while I am _____ [one action], I think about other times when I've felt _____ (⇑).
>
> *I am peaceful, and while I am filing my receipts, I think about other times when I've felt peaceful.*
>
> **Complete this exercise with the other (⇓) feelings and situations you identified until you have worked through the energy-draining list. As you consciously make these links and connections, your subconscious mind is learning to do this process for you. You are building a new habit.**

The old habit of trying to figure out how to solve an uncomfortable situation or event keeps you stuck in unsupportive feelings. Imagine your feelings as the house you live in. When you are in negative situations or engaging in actions that lower your energy, it is as if you were living in a small hut with a leaking roof and no heat in the middle of a storm. You huddle in the corner, upset because you're cold and wet. Trying to figure out why this happened to you is really challenging. Now imagine that across the road is a beautiful, warm, and secure home. It is spacious and is waiting to welcome you. All you need to do is cross the road. Once you're warm and dry inside of this new emotional home, you can then look out the window and decide if there is anything you need to bring from the hut. If there are supportive lessons to be learned, you can go back there from your solid place and get what you need, remembering where you *now* live. You've moved across the road, and now you are *visiting* the other side. Focus on building a strong emotional home for yourself instead of trying to repair the hut.

The Legend of "Two Wolves"

Teachings from many different traditions speak about this concept of duality, and it is eloquently described in the legend of the "Two Wolves." This old story, possibly of Native American origin, has been retold in many ways, and although the exact source is unknown, the message is always the same: there are only two places from which we operate—*love* and *fear,* what I've termed the domains of your Inner Coach and your Inner Critic. Every emotion falls into this simple categorization: one side of the line or the other. There are many eloquent versions of the legend. Here's how I relate it to my students:

> A young boy, who was angry with a school-mate, told his grandfather about the injustice. His wise grandfather understood his anger and replied, "I, too, at times have felt a great hate for those who have taken so much with no sorrow for what they do. But hate doesn't hurt your enemy; it only hurts you and wears you down. Holding on to hate is like swallowing poison and wishing that your enemy would die."

The grandfather continued with his story: "There are two wolves inside each one of us. One is good and lives in harmony with all. He is compassionate and hurts no one. He does not take offense when no offense was intended. He will fight if it is the right thing to do, and he always fights in the right way.

"But the other wolf is full of anger. He fights everyone, all the time, for no reason. He cannot think, because his anger and hate are so great. It is hard to live with these two wolves inside me, for both of them try to dominate my spirit."

The grandfather paused, and his grandson asked, "Which wolf wins?"

The Grandfather wisely replied, "The one I feed."

What Are You Feeding?

Your observations feed your learning, and are most supportive when you are either on the line or have crossed it in the (⇑) direction. You know that when children are upset, the first thing you do is help them feel secure, something you might accomplish with a hug or encouraging words. Identifying your emotions as you sort your experiences into the (⇓) or (⇑) side of the line provides the security to engage your Inner Coach, who, like a loving parent, then steps in to move you over the line. No more having to figure out how; just observe and name the feelings, and your Inner Coach will start doing the rest without your even thinking about it!

When you stop spending time and energy justifying your position using all the specific information your Inner Critic was gathering, and use that gathering ability to support your Inner Coach, you'll find yourself moving easily to the side of the line where you want to live. From that more solid emotional space, what you really want becomes clear, and your path opens up. You are successfully re-patterning your thoughts, making decisions in the direction of your dreams, and manifesting what you want quickly—and with relative ease.

Clients who are new to Belief Re-patterning often tell me that it feels too hard to move to the other side of the line, and I understand. Anything new can seem difficult. However, once they've practiced re-patterning, they find it easy to make this move. What turns a new thought or behavior into a habit is conscious practice. With it, moving to the supportive side of the line will become your habitual thought process.

Right now it may seem easy to slip into fear, doubt, and anxiety, but think about living in those states. You've experienced the hardship and pain of living there. The short-term ease of succumbing to your fears and slipping over the line, even if you are justified in doing so, results in long-term challenges. You have been in the uncomfortable hut and know how it feels to hang out there. Choosing to stay on that side of the line is guaranteed to create more of the same.

Even though it may seem challenging to move over the line, think about living in a supportive emotional space. Knowing that a new choice will bring more positive results than what you're currently experiencing is a powerful motivating factor. Getting through the short-term challenge to open up the possibility of long-term *ease* actually seems *easier*. It is your emotional home; on which side of the line are you building it?

I experience incredible joy when I support my clients in living on the (⇑) side of the line. It's especially gratifying when families begin working together in this way. Janice started seeing me to help her move through some debilitating pain. After her initial re-patterning session, she experienced relief, not only from her physical challenges, but also in the interactions with her preteen daughter and teenage son. Since that time the whole family has moved to the (⇑) side of the line and is living in a stable emotional place, both within themselves and with each other. Janice expresses it this way: "We treasure and appreciate the re-patterning . . . which leads to happier, more peaceful, joyous, productive, healthy, and harmonious lives for each of us individually and for the three of us as a family."

Choose two of the situations from the chart you made in your journal and identify emotions that lift your energy. In these Re-patterning Statements, you'll reinforce those feelings.

RE-PATTERNING STATEMENTS FOR
REINFORCING THE POWER OF THE LINE

I acknowledge fear. I **forgive** myself for believing that I need to continue feeding it. That doesn't support me.

I **forgive** myself for believing that it is challenging to move to the supportive side of the line.

I give myself **permission** to learn to move easily to the side of the line of love.

I give myself **permission** to learn what I need to learn from the fear, and then let it go quickly.

I can live on the side of fear, or I can live on the side of love. I **choose** love.

I consciously **choose** to feed my Inner Coach by sorting my experiences and naming the emotions.

I am **free** to live from the side of love with ease.

My mind **freely** focuses on the feelings of _____ (⇑) and _____ (⇑).

My mind freely focuses on the feelings of <u>peace</u> and <u>connection</u>.

Experiences like _____ and _____ **always** place me on the right side of the line!

Experiences like <u>being in the mountains</u> and <u>reading with Jacob</u> always place me on the right side of the line!

I **acknowledge** supportive emotions like _____
(⇑) and _____ (⇑) throughout my day. That keeps
me focused on the right side of the line!

I **live** on the supportive side of the line and make my
decisions from that place.

Whatever you find easy right now is simply habit. If that habit supports you and moves you in the direction of what you want, keep it and strengthen it! If, however, like most of us, you have some thought habits that you know do not support you, relax and know that all habits can be changed and replaced with new ones. You are proactively training your thoughts to move toward the supportive side of the line. Remember the lesson of the "Two Wolves":

"Which one wins, Grandfather?"

"The one I feed."

Reinforce your Inner Coach by reading the following declaration out loud:

My decision to consistently and consciously feed my peaceful, loving, and kind emotions strengthens my Inner Coach so that it is the dominant voice when I most need it. When I fall onto the other side of the line, feeding negative emotions—whether due to challenging circumstances or because I am tired, hungry, or otherwise stressed—my Inner Coach is there, ready to gently and lovingly nudge me back on track.

There is a line, and you are now consciously choosing which side of it to live from. Congratulate yourself for making the move. You are creating a beautiful emotional home. You deserve it.

✳ ✳ ✳ ✳ ✳

Chapter Eleven

YOUR INNER CONVERSATIONS MATTER

✳   ✳   ✳

"Science and psychology have isolated the one prime cause for success or failure in life. It is [your] hidden self-image. . . ."
— BOB PROCTOR

I begin nearly every presentation I give with the question: "If you spoke to your friends the way you speak to yourself, how many friends would you have?" Think about it. I have posed this question to thousands of people over the last decade. There is no right or wrong answer, but listening to your mind's immediate response will give you instant insight into whether your Inner Critic or your Inner Coach is in charge. If your response is *I'd have lots!* then you have a strong and healthy Inner Coach. If your response is more along the lines of *I'd never speak to my friends like that!* or *I wouldn't have any,* then you would join the majority of people I encounter, and your Inner Critic is creating your self-image and is therefore responsible for the results you're getting in your life.

Re-patterning helps you create a more positive self-image. You may have already noticed bits and pieces of the step-by-step pathway coming to mind at random times. You may have been aware of saying, "I forgive myself for believing . . ." as you awaken from a dream. As you go about your day, you may find the thought *I give myself permission to . . .* coming to your awareness. You'll hear yourself use the phrase "I choose . . ." when speaking with a friend.

While driving to work, you might realize you've been visualizing what you are free to experience in your life. You may also notice your mind *connecting the dots,* bringing memories forward to support your learning, which is the Affirmation stage of Belief Re-patterning. And whether you're consciously aware of it or not, the image you hold of yourself is changing and becoming more supportive. You are surrendering into a more authentic feeling of who you are and what value you bring to your world. Developing your own Inner Coach is the goal. You can and will re-pattern anything you choose.

But does your inner dialogue really matter? After all, it isn't as if you were saying the thoughts out loud. Nobody else hears them; they are just thoughts, right? Thoughts are not *just thoughts.* The way you speak to yourself and the self-perceptions you carry determine the outcomes in your life. Even if you never voiced the thoughts aloud, they appear in your behavior and the way you speak to the people around you. You've seen this in others, and those who come into contact with you see it in you. The wonderful part of this is that you can change your thoughts, and your results will change.

Become a Friend to Yourself

Remember, a belief is a thought held in place by emotions. Focusing on switching the emotion is the most effective way to change our thoughts and build supportive beliefs. Emotions are the language of our bodies and are a universal communicator. Regardless of what language we speak, everyone understands the language of emotion, and we constantly read it through body language.

You are aware of your internal responses to the words of others; now shift the focus. Be aware of your body's response to what you say and think to yourself. Read this aloud and note your internal responses:

It doesn't matter how I talk to myself. It doesn't affect me. I'm just joking around when I tell myself that I'm not good enough or that I don't deserve good things.

You may have a physical response, additional thoughts may pop into your head, or the flash of a memory may cross your mind. The image or voice of an influential person in your life might surface. Observe and listen to your internal responses. These are important indicators of how you speak to yourself. If they move you closer to what you desire, your Inner Coach is strong. Unsupportive responses are the domain of your Inner Critic. This is the kind of feedback you wouldn't say out loud to anyone else, or if you did, you wouldn't feel good about it!

Quick Reflection:

HOW DO YOU SPEAK TO YOURSELF?

Notice whether your Inner Critic or your Inner Coach responds as you read this aloud:

If I spoke to my friends the way I speak to myself, how many friends would I have?

There may be some discomfort as you feel your internal response to this question. Somewhere, in your deep knowing, you're aware that your inner dialogue matters. You know that you're harder on yourself than you would ever be on anyone else, let alone someone you love. Observing and recognizing the hurtful things you say to yourself is the beginning of healing that space within you that doesn't quite feel good enough no matter what you do.

Answer the following questions:

- How do you speak to yourself when you make a mistake or mess up something?

- What is your inner conversation when you achieve something good?

Would you categorize your internal dialogue as generally coming from your Inner Critic (⇓) or your Inner Coach (⇑)? Categorizing supportive responses as "Inner Coach" and unsupportive responses as "Inner Critic" allows you to observe your inner conversations. It actually takes you a step away from the action. Would the people who love and support you whom you listed in "Quick Reflection: Surrender to Who You Really Are" ever speak to you the way you speak to yourself? Would you ever intentionally speak that way to a young child or someone *you* care deeply about? Learn to speak to yourself in a kind and honoring way!

It Makes a Difference

You understand the importance of keeping your thoughts positive, but are you aware of just how damaging it is to beat up on yourself? Most people haven't made the connection that their own negative thoughts, directed inwardly, are extremely harmful. When we allow our inner voices to engage in conversations that are judging, harsh, and unkind, we unknowingly create more damage to our sense of self than is caused when someone else speaks that way to us.

Intellectually we recognize that judging, harsh, and unkind words reveal more about the person uttering them than the individual to whom they are directed; however, when these comments elicit an emotional response, that feeds our beliefs about ourselves. When we send an unkind message, we often wish there were a *rewind* switch. When we're on the receiving end, we wish there were a *delete* button. Either way our minds often take what has been said and hit the continuous *replay* button. We run the words over and over and over in our minds, embedding the negative expressions into our subconscious. Once embedded, these messages reinforce our beliefs about who we are and create our self-image.

You noticed how it felt when you really connected your inner response with the memories of those who have put you down. Whenever you put yourself down, your body, mind, and spirit actually respond more strongly than if those same words were coming from someone else. You can't ignore your own words or walk away from yourself. You can't stop listening to *you*. Your personally directed, unsupportive thoughts become part of the content of the internal tapes that play continuously in your subconscious, and your Inner Critic surfaces with them at inconvenient times, causing you to wonder where they came from.

The comments and observations in your inner conversations may have come from someone else originally, but now they are coming from you. Your Inner Critic adopted and adapted the put-downs and judgments of others. Your Inner Coach adopted and adapted the kind and loving words and actions of others. Your subconscious is constantly playing a tape about who you are. The glorious truth is that you can consciously rewrite, change, turn down the volume on, or erase the Inner Critic tapes. You can consciously make tapes for your Inner Coach, turn up the volume, and increase the frequency of play. You have control over the way you play those tapes. You may feel as if they run you, but you are learning to run *them*. You decide, and then you practice.

You can use Re-patterning Statements to get unstuck, and also to strengthen positive learning. Be present to the responses of your body, mind, and soul as you breathe after saying each of the following statements out loud. In your mind, sort your responses with a (⇓) feeling when your Inner Critic surfaces, and a (⇑) feeling when your Inner Coach appears. If no thought or feeling surfaces when you say a statement, it usually indicates agreement, so view those responses as an (⇑) answer as well.

RE-PATTERNING STATEMENTS FOR SELF-ENCOURAGEMENT

I **forgive** myself for all the times I judged myself in the past.

I give myself **permission** to encourage myself.

I can judge myself, or I can encourage myself; I **choose** to encourage myself.

I am **free** to practice encouraging myself as I would a friend.

I **know** how to encourage others. I'm ready to encourage myself the way I did _____ (N) yesterday.

I **am** becoming conscious of the importance of encouraging myself in my inner conversations.

You already have the skills and abilities you need to change those internal tapes that have caused huge damage to your sense of self. Encouraging yourself will shape your inner conversations and change the self-perception that is stored in your subconscious, reflected in your attitude, displayed through your speech and behavior, and then reinforced through your observation of the results. It is all learning, and you are a learning machine. The way you speak to yourself matters. It's the *only* thing that matters, because it affects everything else. It deserves your attention!

For this next exercise, you'll need your journal. You'll be observing your self-image and changing the tapes of your Inner Critic while reinforcing those of your Inner Coach.

Try This One! Practice:

DESCRIBE YOURSELF

In your "Quick Reflection: Intro" at the beginning of the book, you wrote down what you believe to be true about yourself. Set a timer for 60 seconds and add to that list. Write down in your journal as many descriptors as you can. No explanations, judging, or comparing—just list what comes to mind with this question: *What qualities and attributes define me?* Then categorize the descriptors you've listed as Inner Coach (⇑) or Inner Critic (⇓).

One time when I did this exercise, I wrote down "procrastinator" as a descriptor. I probably would not call a loved one a procrastinator. I would word it in a more encouraging way: "You take on so many things that it's sometimes hard for you to get it all done."

Say these two ways of describing the same behavior out loud, breathing each in and being aware of your body's responses:

"I am a procrastinator."

"I take on so many things that it's sometimes hard for me to get it all done."

Everyone has areas in need of growth and improvement, so if your Inner Critic made any (⇓) observations as you described yourself, rewrite the descriptors in a more encouraging and supportive way.

Say both your rewritten (⇓) observation and your encouraging (⇑) one out loud, breathing and *feeling into* your body's responses.

Becoming aware of the feelings that result from how you speak to yourself clears the way for you to increase your positive self-image. After all, you wouldn't hang out with someone who put you down and spoke unkindly to you, and you spend all of your time with yourself! Your inner dialogue creates your self-concept, more so than the thoughts, actions, and comments of others.

I used to focus a great deal of time and energy on wondering what others thought of me, until I came to the understanding that I cannot control how or what others think. I can gain complete control over what I think about myself, and since what I think about myself makes a difference to the quality of my life, I decided to consciously practice simple patterns of becoming aware of, sorting, and then switching my emotions. Because of the way the mind works, I knew that doing so would affect how my subconscious would play the tapes, and then the *control* would become automatic.

How you think about yourself matters. Observe your internal dialogue when you declare this out loud: "I'm learning to speak to myself the way I speak to my friends, and it is making a positive difference in my life!"

It Has to Be Real

Many people, when questioned about their inner dialogue, raise an eyebrow and respond, "Oh, those voices—I just ignore them." This comment is often accompanied by a nervous cough, a physical indication of an attempt to repress negative thoughts.

Not expressing your true self causes frustration and anger, which creates more negative self-talk. Because the inner voice must be heard, if it is suppressed and ignored, it will find its way out in times of stress. We've all experienced our inner voices leaping out at inopportune times. They manifest as judging comments at work that can damage a collegial relationship, harsh words with a partner that can destroy trust, or unkind observations to a child that affect his or her self-concept for years. We've all received and delivered thoughts that would have been better left unsaid.

You may have noticed that the more you ignore the Inner Critic, the louder and more insistent it becomes, and the more likely that it will be outwardly expressed at the wrong time. Your Inner Coach may have fallen silent from being pushed aside and stuffed down until it is left mute. The leap from ignored inner voice to expressed outer voice usually occurs when we are stressed, hungry, overtired, or under attack.

Positive self-talk can't just be *happy talk*. Pretending that everything is good when it isn't doesn't work. You've probably tried that. I know I have, and what usually results is a sarcastic or judging comment. Those Inner Critic comments can undo the good of the positive affirmations.

Let me explain it this way: You see a close friend who asks, "How are you?" You reply enthusiastically, "Super—couldn't be better!" Meanwhile your Inner Critic says, *As if. My life is in shambles, and I haven't got a clue how I'll make my mortgage payment this month. I'm lying to myself, and now I'm lying to my friend.* The Inner Critic's observations may be true, but they aren't kind. You are reinforcing the beliefs that you are both a victim and a liar. A kinder, yet still true, response to the same friend might be, "It's rough right now, but I am confident that things are turning around. Thanks for asking." The reinforced beliefs are: *I am confident and grateful.*

RE-PATTERNING STATEMENTS FOR AUTHENTICITY

I **forgive** myself for believing that I have to pretend or say things that aren't true for me.

I give myself **permission** to be true to me in a kind and caring way.

I consciously **choose** to be true to me.

I am **free** to be true to myself.

I **was** true to myself in a kind way **when** I _____
[past situation].

I **am** building my ability to be true to myself in a kind
and caring way.

It takes concentration to always answer in a way that
is supportive of you. With practice, Belief Re-patterning
builds your Inner Coach's ability to automatically respond positively so that you no longer need to consciously concentrate. You'll experience tangible results.
You'll notice how your energy shifts when you bring
awareness to the way you think and speak. It's not about
pretending, or happy talk; it is about finding ways to
support you that are true to you.

Joan had experienced challenges with ongoing depression, which she treated with years of counseling,
medical solutions, and alternative therapies. Ten years
ago she had a few sessions with me and wrote a long
letter of gratitude that included this explanation: "Belief
Re-patterning has been the single most effective technique that I have experienced to quickly overcome self-
defeating behaviors and move forward in my personal
life. It has enabled me to uncover the real me and to begin to live my life with power." Through re-patterning,
Joan learned to shift her inner conversations to be more
compassionate and caring, and as a result, she is now
much gentler with herself.

If you're not receiving what you want in your life—if
your dreams are not becoming reality—change the story

that you tell yourself about who you are to something more positive. The concept is simple, and implementing the change can be as well! Rewrite in a kinder way what you've been saying to yourself.

Where Did the Story Come From?

Our sense of who we are does come from what others say to us, but only partially. Where our self-concept really develops is in what we *tell ourselves* about what others say about us. It's the replaying and the validation we give to what others say that supports or damages our sense of self. The journey of life really is about coming to know who you truly are and creating the best *you* possible.

We've all used the mind's magnificent ability to analyze *what* has happened or wonder *why* it happened. Focusing your thoughts on an observant and creative place may seem like something new. It's actually completely natural for everyone; you just may not have been consciously doing it. You were born observant and creative. Along the way you began to judge yourself. You were not born judging yourself or others. This is good news, because anything that is learned can be *undone and relearned* in a different way. The judging, doubt, and worry are all learned, and learned behavior can be changed.

Your desire to learn and grow is built in. You may have veered off course by paying more attention to the fear and doubt, but your internal wiring, *your very life,* is wired for growth. Think about it. A baby reaches out with curiosity. A toddler pulls himself up to a standing position and grins. A preschooler dreams of being an astronaut or a teacher, and his play enacts those dreams. You were that baby, toddler, and preschooler, and you are wired to learn and grow. With positive, supportive encouragement, children grow in positive and supportive ways. With put-downs and harsh words, they become stifled, and constant fear stunts their emotional growth.

When my niece, Lyla, was 18 months old, her parents were renovating. A long weekend was coming up, and I offered to take Lyla for all three days so that they could focus on the project. When I arrived early Saturday morning, Lyla came running excitedly to the door with her shoes in hand, grabbed her jacket, hugged her mom and dad, and headed for my car. I buckled her into her car seat, got in the car myself, and looked at her in the rearview mirror. With a smile that went from ear to ear, Lyla said, "Dance!" That was my cue to hit the tunes, and we were on our way, singing along to her favorite CD. We went to the post office, got some groceries, and headed for the park to feed the ducks and play on the slide. Lunch was at my place, and then we read a couple of stories, snuggled in my big bed, and had a nap. All too soon, the day was done, and I drove her home.

Sunday morning Lyla greeted me with a little less excitement, but we jumped in the car and did our usual routine. I looked in the rearview mirror; she gave me a weak smile and said, "Dance," with little enthusiasm. Fortunately as the music started, she perked up, and another great day followed.

Monday morning, day three, Lyla was quiet when I arrived. She'd figured out that another day with Auntie Suze meant a day without her parents. I tucked her into the car seat, knowing that she was fighting her emotions. I hopped in, looked in the rearview mirror, and saw a very pouty lip and big tears forming. You know that place with kids. I had three seconds to divert her attention or I was in for a full-blown emotional meltdown. I turned and faced her and began singing, "I love Lyla, I love Lyla! She's a good girl, and she's funny! We go to the park and play, feed the ducks, and go on the slide."

She was a bit taken aback by this, but listened curiously.

I continued, "I love Lyla, I love Lyla! Go to the store and buy groceries, pick up the mail, drive the car and sing and laugh, and I love Lyla!"

She was starting to smile and nod her head.

I was on a roll: "I love Lyla, I love Lyla! Go to my house, watch TV, snuggle, read a book, have lunch and nap, and I love Lyla!"

It wasn't an award-winning songwriting effort, but it worked. It shifted her thoughts to the fun we always have, and we were on our way! I dropped her off that evening; whispered, "I love Lyla," into her ear; and promised I would see her in four "big sleeps," as I would be taking her the next weekend as well.

Saturday morning I arrived at 7:30. Lyla enthusiastically grabbed her shoes and coat. Her mom told me she had jumped out of bed, excited about getting ready for our day together. She was in such a hurry to get out the door that I had to remind her to hug her mom and dad good-bye. I was relieved that Monday morning's challenge was gone, and smiled as I looked in the rearview mirror. She grinned back and started singing, "I love Lyla! I love Lyla!" We both laughed, and I made up a couple of new verses about the adventures in store.

When I dropped her off after an action-packed day, I told her parents about Lyla singing to me that morning. My brother began to laugh. "You've just solved the mystery of the week!" Apparently the past few days every time Lyla was in her crib she was singing what sounded to him like the old Meow Mix commercial. When I made up the song, that was the tune that surfaced from my memory! She was singing, "I love Lyla," over and over again before she went to sleep and when she woke up. It sounded to them like "La-la-la-la," and they couldn't figure out how she knew the tune since the commercial had aired years before she was born. We had a great laugh about it. How very wise the little ones are! Lyla had learned to soothe herself with positive thoughts.

Please hear me: I wasn't being the knowing aunt who tried to help my niece build a positive self-image. I hadn't carefully planned what I was going to sing to her. I was simply trying to shift Lyla's focus from missing her parents to the fun we were going to have. I helped her *flip her switch,* but she was the one who kept reinforcing the supportive thoughts by singing the song. Lyla is now three and frequently makes up new verses. And whenever she is upset, I hum the song. It works every time!

* * *

What *song* are you singing about yourself? What thoughts are you replaying over and over in your mind?

You were once a child. You heard positive and encouraging words, and you heard harsh and unsupportive ones. You were hugged, loved, and cuddled; and you were hit—whether physically, mentally, or emotionally. You developed thought patterns accordingly. Those thought patterns became your beliefs about yourself. Because *you* built those beliefs, *you* can change them. You have the ability to learn anything, and doing so changes the very fiber of your being.

Each of us has had nasty, hurtful things said to us by others in the past. Some of these memories are buried deep, and we aren't consciously aware of the damage. You may intellectually understand that your parents and teachers did the best they could with the skills and abilities they had, but the sting of the emotional residue may remain in your body and soul, hooking you in when you least expect it. These are the memories that feed the Inner Critic. Similarly, you have memories of loving and supportive things that were said to you. You may have hung on to these treasures to guide you through tough times, and repeated some of them to your own children. Your Inner Coach is nurtured by these memories.

I remember being told both loving and harsh things, and often the messages were mixed:

> "Don't get too big for your britches."
> "You can do anything you set your mind to."

"Nobody thinks like that; are you crazy?"
"I believe in you."
"You talk too much."
"What will the neighbors think?"

Quick Reflection:

RECALL WHAT YOU WERE TOLD AS A CHILD

What do you remember being told as a child? Write a list in your journal, and then categorize each memory as supportive (⇑) or unsupportive (⇓). Reinforce the supportive memories by saying them out loud, breathing deeply, and thanking yourself after each one. If you remember who said this to you, thank that person as well. Here's what I mean:

I can hear my dad telling me, "You can do anything you set your mind to." I am grateful to myself for learning this, and I am grateful to my dad for saying this *[deep breath in and out]*.

Reinforce all the supportive memories in this way, and then switch the perspective of the (⇑) phrases: *you* becomes *I* or *me*, and *your* becomes *my*. These examples will guide you:

You can do anything you set your mind to.	⇒	I can do anything I set my mind to.
I believe in you.	⇒	I believe in me.

There is incredible power in *I* statements. Using *I* in front of or *my* beside any idea sends a strong message to your subconscious. These words carry powerful energy, and your mind uses this information to form your self-concept. Your Inner Coach will get stronger as you write your supportive memories using *I* and *me,* and then say them aloud. You will feel your energy shift!

When you were a child, you absorbed everything that was said to and about you. Some of those things conflicted with each other, and some of them were more about the person who said them than about you. As an adult you have the opportunity to decide which of those observations you'll treasure and which to let go. You have the right to develop yourself in whatever direction you choose. Take personally what feels right, true, and kind. Everything else is there for you to learn from.

Your beliefs permeate your work and social life. Your relationship with yourself is reflected in your relationships with colleagues, friends, and family. What song are you singing yourself to sleep with at night? What are your first thoughts of the morning? Switch them to something more positive and watch as your day unfolds.

Consciously Changing Your Self-Image

This next set of Re-patterning Statements will call forth the voice of your Inner Coach and reinforce it.

For the Affirmation stage of this next set of statements, you'll need a supportive example of a time when you helped someone learn something. Here's what I mean:

> Specific person: *My grandson Jacob*
> Specific thing I helped him learn: *To crawl*

RE-PATTERNING STATEMENTS
FOR SUPPORTING YOURSELF

I **forgive** myself for believing that old hurtful thoughts define who I am.

I recognize that those old thoughts have held me back and kept me stuck; I give myself **permission** to move forward.

I can hang on to those old thoughts, or I can learn from them; I **choose** to learn what I can from them and then let the rest go.

I am **free** to learn to define myself in ways that are supportive.

I **know** how to support others in their learning; I helped _____ [Jacob] learn how to _____ [crawl].

I **am** supportive of others, like _____ [Jacob].

I **give** myself the same support that I gave _____ [Jacob] when he/she was learning to _____ [crawl]. I **am** supportive.

Try This One Practice:

TRANSFORM CHILDHOOD MESSAGES

Now that you've encouraged your Inner Coach, take a look at the memories you listed in the last Quick Reflection that may have contributed to any self-doubt you may carry. You've used your Inner Coach to build a solid place, and now you can more effectively observe the things that were said to you that hurt you at the time and may still sting. In your journal, reframe the memories that haven't supported you, and re-pattern them into something that will contribute to a more positive self-image. You get to decide what works for you. Gently and carefully re-record the tape, one (⇓) memory at a time. With the observant perspective of your Inner Coach, talk yourself through what you would honestly say to a friend if he or she had been told this by someone else.

I remember being told "Nobody thinks like that; are you crazy?" If someone said the same thing to a friend of mine, I would probably respond with something like, "I don't think you are crazy. I know that you look at things differently, but that doesn't make you crazy. It makes you unique. I like the way you look at things differently; it's interesting. Many creative thinkers are misunderstood. You aren't crazy; you are a unique and creative thinker." With a friend, I would never say, "They're right; you are crazy! You are right off your rocker, ready for the institution. No one is ever going to believe you! You are just weird and nuts, and should just shut up!" This wouldn't happen, yet this is pretty close to what I used to say to myself before I began training my Inner Coach to support me as a great friend would.

Try this now with each of the (⇓) memories you listed in the previous Quick Reflection. Use your journal to write down what you would say to convey the message in a kind and caring way. Then write the original (⇓) phrase you remember beside the new (⇑) nugget, with the one you're moving away from on the left and the one you're moving toward on the right:

Nobody thinks like that; are you crazy?	⇒	You are a unique and creative thinker.

And now, turn up your energy by changing the supportive statement to first-person perspective.

You are a unique and cre-ative thinker.	⇒	I am a unique and creative thinker.

As you write your *I* statements in your journal, say them out loud. If your Inner Critic takes exception, use some Re-patterning Statements:

I **forgive** myself for believing that I am _____ (⇓).

I give myself **permission** to stop defining myself as _____ (⇓).

I give myself **permission** to begin defining myself as _____ (⇑).

I can define myself as _____ (⇓) or _____ (⇑), and I consciously **choose** _____ (⇑).

I am **free** to define myself as _____ (⇑).

I **saw** myself as _____ (⇑) **when** I _____.

I **am** _____ (⇑).

Using the Re-patterning Statements in this way will quiet the protests of your Inner Critic.

All inner voices are supportive when we become observant. Even the harsh and judging ones will point us to a helpful new awareness when we step out of the victim place of believing the judgment, and into the (⇑) place of learning and growth. Attempting to control, ignore, silence, or put down the Inner Critic makes the thoughts stronger and louder. Learning to use both the Inner Critic and Inner Coach to support personal development is effective.

You are not your Inner Critic. Those thoughts don't define you. They are simply inner thoughts and awareness reflecting back to previous learning: the things you heard or experienced at some earlier point in time that became part of your memories, and therefore part of you. Both the Inner Critic and the Inner Coach are the expressions of all of that learning. Some of those inner thoughts are helpful, and some pull you off track. Words or actions that have enough repetition and emotion attached, whether supportive or unsupportive, became your learned beliefs about yourself and the way the world works. Your thoughts and inner conversations are simply retrieving the memory and bringing it to consciousness.

Transform your inner voices from unconscious tug-of-wars to thoughtful, conscious, and creative conversations. Teach yourself how to use positive self-talk on a subconscious level by practicing it consciously. Use your inner comments to continue to make positive changes, realize new results, and shift your beliefs about yourself. You're learning to speak to yourself the way you would speak to a friend. You will always have conversations with yourself; they might as well be compassionate, encouraging, conscious, supportive, purposeful, and authentic.

Forgiveness, Permission, Choice, Freedom, Affirmation, and Surrender—this is the step-by-step pathway for changing the way you speak to yourself and moving you effortlessly and automatically across the line.

※　※　※　※　※

Chapter Twelve

EXERCISE YOUR INNER COACH, ACKNOWLEDGE YOUR INNER CRITIC

✳   ✳   ✳

"You, yourself, as much as anybody in the entire universe, deserve your love and affection."

— BUDDHA

All of us have the ability to define who we are. Fortunately you don't need to have a degree in psychology or experience life-altering challenges to learn to define yourself in positive and supportive ways; you just need to let go of being a victim of anyone or anything. What is the opposite of that victim space for you? It might be feeling worthy or deserving. It might be strength or empowerment, or feeling appreciated, valued, or nurtured. I don't know, but *you* do. Deep inside you know how you want to feel and what is on the opposite side of the line from that victim place. You may have tried to silence your Inner Critic and discovered that this only works for a short time. Now you're beginning to listen to and appreciate your Inner Critic, whose comments can point you in the right direction.

You've been building a strong and secure emotional home, and have begun spending more and more time in this supportive place. From here it's much easier to look back into the victim space you've experienced. You'll be fine. There will be some gems of wisdom and real insights under the floorboards of the old, leaky emotional hut you've been living in. You've laid the groundwork and built a positive foundation on which to stand and survey how you have felt like a victim in the past.

Tom Paxton, one of the iconic folksingers of the past 50 years, was recently performing at a 40th-anniversary celebration of the Calgary Folk Club. His comments about reviewing the past really struck me. He said, "Nostalgia is great; it's just not good to stare." There's nothing wrong with looking back, especially to remember the positive and supportive things you've experienced. It's also useful to examine some of the things that hurt you or were painful. You aren't going back there to live, and you aren't going to *stare* into the pain. You are simply observing the place of *not good enough* or *wrong* and letting your Inner Coach ask, *What do I want instead of that feeling?*

I imagine that just about everyone has experienced coaches or teachers who operated from the (⇓) side of the line. As adults we recognize that bullying young people by putting them down and yelling doesn't work. When we were younger, we may have accepted their harsh words as truth; after all, they were the tall people in charge, and we paid attention. Sometimes the consequences of not listening were painful, which caused us to really take their words to heart.

You were taught to listen to your elders. Their comments became the fragments you pulled together to create your self-concept. You may not have seen or interacted with those individuals for years, but in their absence, your mind has repeated their words, reinforcing the emotion you felt and re-creating what happened. You might not consciously remember the specifics, and fortunately you don't need to. Your subconscious is holding the energy, and relays the memory through emotion. You don't need to remember and relive the experiences consciously. You recognize the emotion, and you know which side of the line it is on.

As an adult, you've become more discerning about letting others define you, yet without a strong, supportive Inner Coach, you may still let the words and observations of others damage your self-image, especially if you have a strong pattern of experiencing that in your childhood.

You wouldn't consciously choose to work with a coach or teacher who used negative control methods. You know it doesn't work for you that way and that encouragement and kindness get much more effective results. Nurturing your Inner Coach is about directing to yourself that same encouragement and love that you give so easily to others. You operate from the supportive side of the line with those you care about.

If you wonder why you've had challenges with making positive changes in your life, perhaps it could be that you've beaten yourself up, put yourself down, and generally not treated yourself well. You may have been operating in your own mind from the ($\Downarrow$) side of the line. You wouldn't spend a lot of time with an acquaintance who didn't show you understanding and compassion, you wouldn't hire a personal trainer who discouraged you and called you out in sarcastic ways, you wouldn't enjoy working for a boss who didn't value your contribution or didn't care about your well-being . . . yet you may have unconsciously been letting your Inner Critic get away with these old habits.

Do you wonder why you're so hard on yourself? There is one simple answer: you learned that way of being to the point where it became a pattern. As an adult you may seek out those who have the same patterns of control as the influential people in your childhood, further reinforcing the abusive self-talk you adopted early on. In the absence of those who put you down, silenced your creativity, or unkindly teased you, you may have taken up the cause, being harder on yourself than you would ever be on anyone else. If you have treated yourself this way, it's because somewhere in your life, you learned that behavior. Now you can re-pattern it.

A great deal of personal development focuses on examining all the reasons why something isn't working and then trying to fix it. People focus their energy on identifying and releasing blocks, and examining issues. My clients often say, "What's wrong with me is . . ." or "I have an issue with . . ." What we focus on expands. What we think about we create. Sometimes we feel dumped on by others, and then we sort through the resultant pile of stuff. Most of the time it isn't even our stuff, yet we accept that because it has landed in our laps, it's our responsibility.

Addressing the Inner Critic

Regardless of how your Inner Critic shows up, you know that's who is in charge when you focus on what you didn't do or how badly you messed up. Along with the accomplishments and achievements, there will be some wrong turns and false starts. There will be times when you don't say something but wish you could, and times when you do say something you wish you *hadn't.* Then your Inner Critic, masquerading as reality, may surface in an attempt to build the case that life is full of problems and trials.

Listening to that Inner Critic can provide some helpful information, but believing those thoughts will spiral you right into feeling like a victim. You can beat yourself up over a decision, or your Inner Coach can support you by saying something like, *I didn't make a bad decision. I made the best decision I could at the time, given the information I had. It didn't work out the way I thought it would, so now I have the opportunity to make a new decision.* The truth is that you create your reality by your response to whatever is happening. Life does present challenges that can be tough to handle, but an overactive Inner Critic will make them tougher by overdramatizing, playing them over and over in your mind, or jumping to conclusions. Whether you're blaming yourself or others, being a victim is not where you want to be. Your Inner Critic isn't the bad guy here; it just needs the balancing influence of a strong Inner Coach to provide guidance in how to support you instead of shut you down.

Through your self-talk, you either learn and move forward, or open the door to the victim place and make yourself at home. Our inner conversation either victimizes or empowers us. Our perceptions color every experience and determine on which side of the line we spend our time. Some see the doughnut, and some see the hole, but the doughnut remains the same. Some see opportunity, and some see problems, but the event is the same.

The gifts you were born with and the environment you experienced as a child contribute to your way of being in the world. But what really makes all the difference between a life of misery and a life well lived is what you do with what you have. How you experience your life is determined by how you see yourself.

Your feeling victimized by people, events, or circumstances outside of yourself is always compounded by your self-talk. No one can make you a victim. Your own beliefs about who you are define you. Those beliefs are delivered to your conscious mind through your Inner Critic or Inner Coach. The messages of the Inner Critic victimize *you*, not your situation or circumstances. Letting go of feeling like a victim as quickly as possible whenever you feel yourself going down that path involves attending to your Inner Critic to uncover what the message is pointing to, rather than victimizing yourself by believing it.

Imagine that your doorbell is ringing and outside there's a delivery person with a truck parked on your driveway filled with problems, issues, and negative energy. Just because someone rang your doorbell does not mean that you need to accept everything into your emotional home. You can refuse delivery. There's no need to *return to sender.* Just gently smile, decline the delivery, and close the door. It's your door and your emotional home, and you choose who and what you invite to join you there.

Not all deliveries that appear to be from the (⇓) side of the line are actually unsupportive. You now know how to re-pattern the emotional energy of any situation from one side of the line to the other. Your front doorbell rings again. You open the door and see an enormous dump truck, filled to the top with manure. You wouldn't think of asking the driver to back the truck up to your front door and leave the contents in your living room. You may, however, realize that this delivery is exactly what you need to nourish the fabulous vegetable garden you are creating in your backyard, so you redirect the truck to the back alley, open the gate, and get the fertilizer you need to create your dreams.

The delivery of the manure is neither (⇓) nor (⇑), and neither are the events of your life. It's how and where you choose to let the delivery land that determines whether it is a big pile of waste or fertilizer for your dreams. Each of us has experienced the power of something that seemed devastating at the time transforming our lives in an incredibly supportive manner. Re-patterning shortens the time frame of the transformation.

Janine and her husband, Carl, were living in an idyllic mountainside location. They'd left the city and decided to transform their summer cabin into a year-round home. A friend as well as a client, Janine worked with me over the phone to re-pattern her beliefs around allowing abundance into her life. She refocused her mind on seeing herself as worthy and deserving of abundance. Several days later we were on a follow-up call when she looked out the window to see dump truck after dump truck emptying piles of dirt into the ravine in front of her home. She started to panic.

Just then, her husband arrived home grinning from ear to ear. She asked if she could call me back. Ten minutes later, Janine was on the phone again, but this time she was laughing.

She and Carl had spent months trying to figure out how to place their dream home on their lot. Working around the ravine had been the big challenge. That morning Carl had been on his way into town, and while he was trying to turn left onto the main road, he was held up as several dump trucks full of dirt passed by, heading down into the valley. An idea flashed in his mind. He immediately switched his turn signal, turned right, and began driving up the mountain, passing more dump trucks until he arrived at their source. A new development was under construction, and Carl found the project foreman. The crew was digging basements and leveling lots. They had literally tons of earth to move, and the foreman mentioned how expensive it was to truck all that dirt down into the valley and then pay for disposal.

Janine's husband shared this idea: bring the dirt to his ravine and dump it there. They would save not only the disposal fees, but also time and gas. The foreman immediately saw the benefit of Carl's idea and radioed the driver of one of the dump trucks, intercepting him on his way down the mountainside. Carl gave the driver exact directions to his ravine and told them he was on his way to meet them. By the time he arrived home, the five trucks had already dumped their loads into the ravine, and Carl went into the house totally excited to tell Janine of the win-win solution he had created!

As Janine related the story, we both laughed at how abundance doesn't always take on the form you imagine. While Janine was imagining money coming into their bank account so that they could build the home they desired, other forces were at work!

She told me the trucks were going to keep coming all day. We figured out the price of buying and trucking one load of fill to their place, and realized that in the space of one day, they had manifested thousands of dollars in dirt! Although this was not what she'd imagined, it was an answer to the challenges they'd been experiencing on the way to their dreams. The *problem* for them and the developers had been transformed into a *solution* that worked for everyone.

Rather than push against what you don't want, imagine that everything that arrives at your door is there to support your dreams and desires. Instead of actively problem solving, be open to seeing solutions. No one intentionally holds themselves back, but every one of us has pushed against what we don't want in an attempt to create what we *do* want. Usually the harder we push, the harder whatever is in our way pushes back.

Let Go and Let God

"Let go and let God" is a popular affirmation in the recovery movement. Even though I understood the wisdom of handing over problems and trials to a higher power, I used to really have challenges with doing so. I believe in personal responsibility, and just handing over everything to a power greater than I was seemed like relinquishing my responsibility. It felt out of alignment. I had gotten over the need to be in control. I even used a coffee mug that had a variation on the Dan Millman quote (probably originally from another author, Larry Eisenberg): "If you want peace of mind, I suggest you resign as manager of the Universe." I would sort of hand things over, but I kept worrying about them because I thought I had to be responsible. It was a crazy place to live in, but I found myself there for some time, until one day I realized what part was my responsibility.

I was working on a project for a nonprofit organization and had been assigned a large task that was pivotal to the success of the organization. I told the director, Beth, how I appreciated her hands-off approach. She replied, "I delegated it to you because I believed you could do the job well. Why would I meddle with a good thing?" And then I realized that Beth's responsibility was to hold the vision of the organization, put in place the people who could accomplish whatever needed doing, and support them by believing in them. In previous work situations, I had often been asked to do something and then been driven crazy by the supervisor's continual checking in on me, telling me how I should be doing things, and getting in the way of my just doing what I knew how to do.

A very big penny dropped. Even though I'd handed over things in my life to my higher power, I was hovering around, trying to make things look a certain way or happen in a specific manner, or deciding that I had a better idea, just like those supervisors who had driven me crazy. I was getting in the way of letting my higher power do what it knows how to do better than any way I could come up with. I realized my part in the co-creation of my life at that moment. My responsibility is like Beth's: hold the vision and believe. In my personal affairs, my responsibility is to keep my thoughts on the supportive side of the line, allowing the magic of life to work its power. I didn't need to relinquish responsibility; I simply needed to reframe it!

RE-PATTERNING STATEMENTS
FOR REFRAMING RESPONSIBILITY

I **forgive** myself for believing that life is about solving problems.

I give myself **permission** to focus on how I want to feel, and move myself consciously to the supportive side of the line.

I give myself **permission** to let go of trying to figure out how I will solve problems.

I **choose** to consciously create and expand supportive feelings.

I am **free** to focus on my way of being. That is my responsibility.

Every time I focus on feeling how I want to feel, my life works.

I engage the magic of life by **being** responsible for my feelings and moving them to the supportive side of the line.

Did your Inner Critic respond to any of these statements? If so, a simple acknowledgment will often quiet this voice: *I hear you, and I understand that this is how it has been until now.* Follow up that acknowledgment with a statement of intention: *I am changing what I am responsible for, beginning now.* Whenever your Inner Coach responds, acknowledge the supportive response with heartfelt self-gratitude. Every response your mind brings will take you closer to what you desire when you assume responsibility for using both your Inner Critic and your Inner Coach to move yourself gently to the supportive side of the line.

The first time I heard the expression "Mind your own vibration" was at a Michael Losier workshop. I loved Michael's twist on "Mind your own business," and the phrase stuck with me. Your vibration is reflected in your body language, sending strong messages not only to other people, but also into the Universe. The Law of Attraction responds to your vibration, which is the energetic field that you emit that changes according to your emotions. Belief Re-patterning is a simple way to increase your positive vibration. Learning to *mind your own vibration* by keeping your thoughts on the supportive side of the line works. Working hard at keeping your thoughts positive or forcing yourself to be happy when you just don't feel that way comes from the wrong side of the line and therefore doesn't work. The way you feel about anything is reflected in your words and reactions, even when you think you're doing a great job of covering up how you feel. The energetic vibration that you emit tells the truth of how you feel. Pretending that you're up when you're not moves you to the unsupportive side of the line, lowering your vibration and feeding your Inner Critic.

I work with a family of three young competitive athletes. They understand the role of a coach, and their mom, Marianne, understands the power of the inner game. We re-pattern together, helping them be responsible for holding the vision of what they are creating and keeping their thoughts on the supportive side of the line. When I first met Marianne, her daughter was a promising skater, but lacked confidence. Marianne described how exercising the Inner Coach over the course of a year affected not only her daughter's skating, but also other areas of her life:

> My daughter started out withdrawn and quiet. The change we saw was amazing. By the end of the summer, she was a new girl. She participates in class at school, is able to partner with different children, and no longer depends on a certain friend. Another great change was in her competitive figure skating. Belief Re-patterning has taught her how to set a goal and

coach herself through it. She spent time every night talking herself through her goal and practicing what Belief Re-patterning has taught her. She achieved her goal and is ready for her next competition!

Consciously exercising your Inner Coach increases your ability to effectively process your emotions and move quickly to the supportive side of the line, allowing your words and actions to come from a genuine place of love. Prepare for this series of statements by bringing to mind three of your personal strengths.

RE-PATTERNING STATEMENTS THAT BALANCE YOUR INNER CRITIC WITH YOUR INNER COACH

I **forgive** myself for believing that it is hard to strengthen my Inner Coach.

I **forgive** myself for believing that it doesn't matter if my Inner Critic is in charge.

I give myself **permission** to exercise my Inner Coach with gentleness and encouragement.

I give myself **permission** to acknowledge my Inner Critic with my Inner Coach.

I **choose** to consciously practice strengthening my Inner Coach.

I **choose** to support myself by introducing one change at a time.

I am **free** to build the habit of listening to my Inner Coach.

I am **free** to acknowledge my strengths and exercise my Inner Coach.

I **know** how to encourage my Inner Coach by focusing on my strengths of _____ (⇑), _____ (⇑), and _____ (⇑).

I **am** raising my vibration by exercising my Inner Coach.

Quick Reflection:

ACKNOWLEDGE YOUR CHANGES

Are you finding that your Inner Coach emerges in your thoughts more often? Have you noticed a change in your relationships, work, or outlook? Have you observed a different way of being? In your journal acknowledge some of the specific changes you're noticing in your life. My friend Adrienne once told me: "It's hard to see the picture when you're inside the frame." You may find it helpful to ask for input from a close friend or family member. As Marianne and her daughter did, you'll discover changes in many more areas than you have consciously re-patterned.

Consciously exercising your mind in this way creates incremental growth. When you start a new physical training program, you know that in the beginning, the changes are subtle, and then one day, you realize that your body is stronger. The same process happens with your mind. You'll realize that you're actually living on the supportive side of the line without thinking about it and that things are working in your favor more often.

Longtime client Joanne expressed her experience in this way: "I like to tell people that Suze saved my life. Before I met her, I no longer felt that life was worth living. After starting to work with her, I noticed moments when I felt happy for no reason. One day I realized that happy was now my normal state of being. I no longer needed a reason to be happy; I just was. Ten years later, I wish for everyone to have a life as full and worthwhile as my life now is."

It's wonderful to receive such an outpouring of appreciation, and I receive Joanne's gratitude with humility. I know what part I was responsible for. I helped her create and hold the vision of what she wanted, and believed she could do it until she'd exercised her Inner Coach enough to not only hold and believe in her vision, but also live it!

Joanne was responsible for consciously choosing to move herself over the line from feeling that life wasn't worth living to feeling happy. She focused her energy on practicing moving her thoughts across the line. She strengthened her Inner Coach. As her Belief Re-patterning practitioner, I was her guide, and the model for developing her own Inner Coach.

Whenever you're learning anything new, it works to focus on your strengths. Learning to love yourself can be a challenging lesson. Love for yourself may be buried under years of regret and pain, but you do love yourself at some level: your willingness to seek out support and make positive change in your life is visible evidence of that. You have the capacity to deepen that love and embrace who you truly are. When you increase your capacity to honor who you are by allowing all of your positive attributes to shine, the change you desire will come. You get to develop yourself as a unique individual by strengthening the things you like about yourself and learning from the things you dislike. Your friends and colleagues are likely already noticing the change in you and may be asking what's going on in your life. You're exercising your Inner Coach, and it shows. Congratulate yourself with gratitude!

Try This On! Practice:

POINT A FINGER OF ACKNOWLEDGMENT

There is a saying that when we point a finger at someone, three are pointing back at us. This usually refers to a finger pointed in blame or judgment, and is designed to help us become aware that when we judge or blame others, there is something we can learn in the situation.

It will likely come as no surprise to you, but I prefer looking at it another way. When we compliment someone, we're actually *pointing a finger* of acknowledgment, and three fingers are pointed back toward us. What I mean is that what I value in others is often something that I already value in myself or that I want to learn and develop. In "Quick Reflection: Surrender to Your Best Self" in Chapter 9, you listed some of the positive influences in your life and what those people would say are your strengths. You used their perspective to become observant about your strengths. Go back to that list in your journal. Beside each name, write the person's positive attributes, and what you value and appreciate about him or her.

Whatever positive quality you notice in another is also within you. It may be a seed waiting to develop or a quality that can be acknowledged. Like attracts like, so if you value honesty in others, it is undoubtedly because *you* are honest. You appreciate the kindness of someone else, because you want to develop that same quality. Connecting your positive attributes to someone who has modeled this for you is a terrific way to strengthen your Inner Coach.

Copy your Affirmation Statements into your journal, inserting the quality or strength (S) and the individual's name (N) in the appropriate spaces, using the italicized examples as models.

I appreciate _____ (S). I'm learning to be _____ (S) from _____ (N).

I appreciate playfulness. I'm learning to be playful from Jacob.

I value _____ (N)'s ability to be _____ (S) and _____ (S). I recognize that same _____ (S) and _____ (S) in myself.

I value Mardelle's ability to be honest and straightforward. I recognize that same honesty and straightforwardness in myself.

In Chapter 8 "Affirmation: Linking the New to the Known," I introduced modeling as a strong form of learning. Support your Inner Coach by closely observing someone who displays the quality you would like to develop. Statements like this will help reinforce your learning from that person's modeling:

I appreciate _____ (N). I'm learning to be _____ (S) and _____ (S) by observing him/her. When I'm not sure how to be _____ (S) and _____ (S), I'll think of what _____ (N) would do and try doing that. If it feels right, I'll keep doing it, and if it doesn't, I'll try something else.

I appreciate Dale. I'm learning to be thoughtful and wise by observing her. When I'm not sure how to be thoughtful and wise, I'll think about what Dale would do and try doing that. If it feels right, I'll keep doing it, and if it doesn't, I'll try something else.

I'm so grateful to _____ (N) for giving me a model for being _____ (S)!

I'm so grateful to Ally for giving me a model for being fun loving!

With these exercises, finger-pointing takes on a whole new perspective! Enjoy building the strength of your Inner Coach by consciously watching and learning from those whom you respect. Rekindle the fun you had as a child observing your world!

It's Easy to Give to Others!

Another fabulous place to learn how to treat ourselves well is by being observant of our own behavior. Often what we easily give to others is something that we wish we could have ourselves. As kids, my brothers gave my dad a football for his birthday. Think about some of the gifts you've given to friends and family over the years, and you'll notice that often they are things that you'd also like! It's natural to give someone else what you'd enjoy yourself, and this applies to both gifts of the heart and material gifts. By observing which of your qualities you easily share with others, you will identify some of the qualities that you could give to yourself, as well as some of the actions that will help you do so.

Quick Reflection:

GIVE TO YOURSELF

In your journal, write down the gifts of the heart that you share easily with people you care about. Attributes like *patience, understanding,* and *love* will help you get your list started. Once you have eight or ten attributes, shift your focus from what you give to how you give it. How do you show others that you care? What do you do? What do you say? Here are some ideas to get you started: *listening, being there for them, making them food, telling them how important they are to me. . . .*

Proactively doing these reflections will help you build Re-patterning Statements that are specific to you. Consciously practicing this will assist your Inner Coach in retrieving examples that support your re-patterning. Insert one or two strengths into the statements you're creating. It's more powerful to create a second statement with additional strengths. However, the more you include names of specific people, the more the statements will actually be reinforced and clarified. You can either write these statements in your journal or say them out loud. You know what best reinforces your learning.

I already know how to be caring and thoughtful to
_____ (N), _____ (N), and _____ (N).
I now choose to give that same care and thoughtfulness to myself.

I already know how to be caring and thoughtful to <u>Mom</u>, <u>Dad</u>, <u>Camille</u>, <u>Charis</u>, and <u>Dave</u>. I now choose to give that same care and thoughtfulness to myself.

I already know how to be _____ (S) and _____
(S) with _____ (N), _____ (N), and _____
(N). I now choose to be just as _____ (S) and
_____ (S) with myself.

I already know how to be <u>attentive</u> and <u>present</u> with <u>Flo</u>, <u>Trudy</u>, and <u>Christie</u>. I now choose to be just as <u>attentive</u> and <u>present</u> with myself.

I'm grateful to _____ (N), _____ (N), and
_____ (N). They have given me a place to practice being _____ (S). I now give that _____ (S) to myself.

I'm grateful to <u>Kathleen</u>, <u>Dale</u>, and <u>Val</u>. They have given me a place to practice being <u>a great friend</u>. I now give that <u>great friendship</u> to myself.

What if you began to more frequently show yourself that you care? What would you do? What would you say? In your journal write some specific examples to support your Inner Coach.

By valuing your strengths and coming from the place of love, you will create a more positive self-image. If your Inner Critic is voicing a concern that you might become egotistical, you can let that go. Egotism comes from the fear side of the line. You're coming from the love side of the line.

Proactively exercising your Inner Coach on a daily basis results in a strong, positive perspective. It raises your vibration, providing personal benefits for you, and produces a positive, profound ripple effect to those around you. Your Inner Coach is behind your new, empowering autopilot program that will bring you to the supportive side of the line every time.

* * * * *

Chapter Thirteen

IT'S ALL PERCEPTION, AND IT'S ALL LEARNED

* * *

"The most powerful thing you can do . . . to change the world is to change your own beliefs about the nature of life, people, and reality, and begin to act accordingly."

— SHAKTI GAWAIN

Now you know how to uncover those old feelings of being a victim and use them to create a stronger self-concept, but if you're like most people, you may be caught up in wondering where those feelings of victimization came from. As I've continually emphasized, trying to figure out the source will keep you stuck in old patterns. You recognize that you developed your beliefs about yourself and the way the world works from a variety of environments, including family, the media, and school. Your self-perceptions are fundamental to the way you experience life, and rather than figure out where the beliefs came from, change them by re-patterning them to something more positive.

When I work with clients, I often re-pattern their beliefs around how they learn because that effects change
in every aspect of their lives. If we truly believe that we
can learn whatever we set our minds to, we will experience life in a very different way than if we believe that
it's hard for us to learn. Life is all about learning, and for
most of us, school was a breeding ground for developing
the negative self-talk that keeps us feeling like victims.

Some kids learn from an abusive parent, sibling, or
schoolmate to build themselves up by putting others
down. We've all witnessed the cruel ways that children
can treat each other, and we've all experienced being put
down or ridiculed at some point. As children become so-
cialized, they learn to treat others with respect, but hit-
ting and name-calling still occur—usually out of sight of
the adults. Then teachers intervene, the fight is broken
up, detentions are assigned, and the "winner" (there's always a winner) serves the detention with a self-satisfied
smirk. His or her self-confidence has been reinforced
through mistreating others.

Even though justice has been delivered, the damage
is done to the recipient of the bullying. The person has
begun to see him- or herself as a *victim,* and that self-perception will continue to be reinforced. Each of us creates
a perception around everything that happens to us, either
consciously or subconsciously. That perception then provides a container for the next experience to fit into.

Teachers address put-downs and bullying in their
classrooms in different ways. I watched strict disciplinar-
ians maintain control, but it felt to me as if the *teachers* were bullying their students, just in more socially
acceptable ways. It may have worked for them, but it

didn't work for me. In my first few years of teaching, I observed teachers who respected their students. It wasn't about developing classroom control or even self-control. It was about building self-confidence and self-respect. When students believe in themselves and respect each other as learners, classrooms become incredible learning environments.

The first week of September was all about getting to know each other and creating context and connections for the students' learning. Together we would create the guiding principles for our classroom, including how the students treated each other as learners. We talked directly about how each of us was personally responsible for our own experiences and how everyone would experience success throughout the year.

I believed in the students' ability to learn and be successful, and we practiced ways of building that belief in them. I encouraged my junior-high students to let go of the idea that they had a problem when they needed help. Instead of "I have a problem," I asked them to say "I have a challenge." I would then respond with "Tell me about the challenge so that we can find a creative solution." Rather than "I need help," they were asked to use "I have a question." I would then respond with "Let's help you find the answer." "I don't understand" became "I'm ready to learn," and "I don't get it" shifted to "Can you please explain it another way?"

For the first couple of weeks, they would roll their eyes, but would humor me and go along with it. By the end of September, they were speaking with each other in similar ways. They had learned that the way they asked for help set them up for success. They came to focus on what they wanted rather than what they didn't want. If the Inner Critic was doing the asking, it was harder. If their questions arose from the Inner Coach, learning came more easily. Creative solutions were much more fun to think about than problems, and the culture of the classroom was established.

When the students stated a problem, they recognized that they began in a hole. That meant they needed time and energy to crawl out of the hole before they could start getting what they wanted. Shifting their perceptions gave them a shortcut to what they needed . . . and *everyone* loves shortcuts! I reminded them that they were placing creative energy wherever their thoughts were focused. When they formed a link between the concept of challenge and the opportunity for creative solution, their thoughts remained on the right side of the line.

Kids label themselves as learners based on their past experiences, and for some of them, those past experiences didn't help them feel good about themselves. So they learned to shift the way they saw themselves as learners:

Inner Critic		Inner Coach
I'm just stupid.	⇒	I haven't learned that. I'm ready to.
I don't know . . .	⇒	I'm curious about . . .
I can't . . .	⇒	Up to now, I haven't . . .
I'm bad at math.	⇒	Math was challenging. I'm ready to get it!

You've labeled yourself as a learner. Do you learn easily, or do you avoid new situations because you find it hard to learn? Is your Inner Critic or your Inner Coach in charge of your perceptions?

Your Perceptions of Yourself as a Learner

Some of your perceptions came from what your teachers and classmates told you. If those perceptions are supportive, hang on to them! If you continue to carry some from your school days that don't support you as an adult, it's time to re-pattern. Teachers are just people, and sometimes they have bad days and say things in hurtful ways that damage their students' self-confidence. What if you've continued to believe something a teacher said on a bad day? What if you could learn and grow past whatever happened that's been feeding your Inner Critic all these years?

My clients are always surprised by the amount of emotion we uncover when we work through some of these old perceptions from their school experiences. Even if you've come to terms with a particular event, the perception you hold may still be playing out in your life. Re-patterning allows you to reclaim your personal power from past situations and circumstances that hurt you. You learned ways of coping and dealing with what others told you. One of them was to decide that the perception was your truth. If the perception is supportive, that's a good thing; however, if you're experiencing difficulties in life or aren't achieving what you want, it's because you're holding an unsupportive perception of yourself as a learner. You can change it, even one you've held on to for years.

I've always enjoyed my good friends Bev and Bob. Their home is my home when I visit their city, and I feel welcomed as part of their family. Years ago their eldest son was having challenges. He was bright and clearly intelligent but just didn't do well at school. This led to low self-esteem, resulting in poor job opportunities when he graduated.

Bev asked me to sit down with her son and do some re-patterning. He wasn't all that keen at first but was willing to indulge his mom and me. Within a few minutes, he was engaged. Through muscle testing, we identified an (⇓) emotion and a time frame. He had been completely unaware of how the beliefs he had formed about himself as a result of an incident in second grade had negatively colored all of his learning experiences since then. An hour later, we had completed the re-patterning. Years later, both he and his parents credit that one session with helping him turn his life around. He is now a trainer for a major corporation and enjoying a wonderful lifestyle.

Quick Reflection:

REFRAME OLD SELF-PERCEPTIONS

The perceptions you subconsciously developed of yourself as a student continue to impact how you learn today. This reflective exercise will reframe those old perceptions that have been in your way. Set up a chart in your journal, as you did in Chapter 10, but this time reflect on your belief about learning and how you learn. Categorize each perception as (⇓) or (⇑), and identify the emotions attached to it.

The next step is to identify the opposite, positive emotions and beliefs for the perceptions that you labeled as (⇓), and then rewrite the old perceptions as supportive (⇧) beliefs. If all of your perceptions of your-self as a learner are already supportive, you can still do the activity and strengthen those supportive beliefs.

Set up this activity in your journal in this way:

Old (⇓) perception: I *believe*   (⇓) Feeling: *stupid*
learning is hard.

Feeling: *stupid*   ⇒   able (⇧)

Belief: *hard*   ⇒   ease (⇧)

New (⇧) perception to build: *Learning comes with ease.*
I feel able.

As you write this new perception, your Inner Critic may have some feedback. Jot it down as well. You can use it as you personalize your Re-patterning Statements.

One of my perceptions that came from my school days surfaced while I was preparing this book. I write well under pressure and am good with deadlines. As a university student I would often complete assignments in the wee hours of the morning, just before the paper was due. I always did exceptionally well, which reinforced that perception. However, through the process of writing the manuscript, I discovered that the perception I learned as a coping mechanism nearly 40 years ago had been taking me off track ever since. I realized that whenever I have a written assignment—be it my monthly newsletter, a new course, an article, or in this case, the manuscript— I work against a deadline. I decided to re-pattern that perception. It no longer serves me. I stopped referring to the book's deadline. The writing began to flow with ease, and an interesting side benefit is that I started arriving early to meetings and events. Isn't it interesting how beliefs permeate every aspect of our lives? Re-patterning a belief in one area will always overflow into others.

Choose one of your off-track self-perceptions about learning that you reworked in the preceding reflection, and insert the responses into these Re-patterning Statements.

**RE-PATTERNING STATEMENTS
FOR PERCEPTIONS ON LEARNING**

I **forgive** myself for believing _____ [old perception].

I give myself **permission** to let go of that old perception; it is in my way.

I can _____ [old perception], or I can create the feeling of _____ (⇑) when I learn. I **choose** to learn with _____ (⇑).

I am **free** to _____ [new perception] and feel _____ (⇑)!

I **know** how it feels to _____ [new perception]. I felt _____ (⇑) when I _____ [specific, true example].

Learning is _____ [new perception] for me, and I **am** _____ (⇑).

You can shift any unsupportive self-perception. With new information and a bit of practice, every learned habit, belief, and perception can be changed. Life presents opportunities to learn every day. You've observed others learning the hard way. Changing your inner conversation will help you see where you might have been making things harder on yourself than was necessary. When you realize that you've created a lot of the pressure and stress you've felt, you will let go of that previous pattern of behavior and choose a new way of being, based on the new belief or perception.

What other ways have you been labeling yourself as a learner that have created stumbling blocks for you? How might it support you to see yourself as curious rather than not knowing? Careful rather than slow? Competent rather than unable? You're training your Inner Coach to look for opportunities to learn, rather than allowing your Inner Critic to focus on problems. This raises your vibration and gives you new energy to fuel your dreams.

Create Your Day Consciously

Let's use an everyday experience to illustrate a way to consciously create how you would rather feel using re-patterning. About an hour ago, I looked up from my writing, sat back in my chair, closed my eyes, and heard my Inner Coach ask, *What am I feeling?*
Tired.
What would I rather feel?
Energized.

With water or food?
No.
With a nap or a walk?
A walk! was the enthusiastic reply.

I looked at the clock and realized I had been sitting at my desk for a couple of hours. I grabbed my coat and went outside, saying Re-patterning Statements out loud to reinforce what I wanted to create and taking a deep breath of fresh air after each one:

I **forgive** myself for believing I need to create tiredness by not taking a regular break.

I give myself **permission** to be energized by walking outside.

I know how it feels to be tired, and I know how it feels to be energized. I am consciously **choosing** to be energized by walking!

I am **free** to energize myself—body, mind, and soul!

I **feel** energized every time I go outside for a walk.

I **am** energized—body, mind, and soul.

I *felt into* the undesired emotion (⇓), linked it to a (⇑) feeling, and then found a way to increase the desired emotion. When I asked myself how I would rather feel, if the answer had been *rested,* the action initiated by the feeling would have been to take a nap rather than go for a walk. The (⇑) emotion informs my action. In other words, the way I want to *be* points me toward the *do.*

Tap into a feeling you've experienced recently that you would like to move away from. Sit comfortably and ask yourself:

1. What am I feeling (⇓)?

2. What would I rather feel (⇑)?

3. What can I do right now to increase the feeling of (⇑) *[action]*?

Then use Re-patterning Statements while doing the action to change your state of being and raise your vibration.

RE-PATTERNING STATEMENTS FOR USE WITH CONSCIOUS ACTIVITIES

I **forgive** myself for believing I need to create _____ (⇓).

I give myself **permission** to feel _____ (⇑) by _____ *[action]*.

I know how it feels to be _____ (⇓), and I know how it feels to be _____ (⇑). I am consciously **choosing** to be _____ (⇑) by _____ *[action]*.

I am **free** to feel _____ (⇑)—body, mind, and soul!

I **feel** _____ (⇑) every time I _____ *[action]*.

I **am** _____ (⇑)—body, mind, and soul.

Do you see how you can use Belief Re-patterning to shift your own energy? Did you notice that the action comes from the emotion you're moving toward?

We've looked at ways to shift your past perceptions, as well as present ones. You've done some proactive strengthening of your Inner Coach and discovered that since all perceptions are learned, they can be re-patterned. Next we'll focus on using Belief Re-patterning as a daily practice to proactively create what you want in the future.

* * * * *

Chapter Fourteen

PUT ON YOUR OWN MASK FIRST

✳ ✳ ✳

"Begin with the end in mind."
— STEPHEN COVEY

You can re-pattern your emotions, thoughts, and actions . . . and also your day! This next practice is easy to integrate into your life, and it creates a habit of nurturing yourself in a unique way and firmly places you on the right side of the line. It reinforces your Inner Coach by re-patterning the way you begin your day.

Do something for yourself first thing every day.

Seriously. It's that simple.

Consider putting yourself first in your day. It makes an incredible difference. I'm not talking about *I always shower and brush my teeth first thing every morning* kind of nurturing. I mean real *feeds your soul* nurturing.

Your Inner Critic may have already started listing all the things you have to do before you run out the door, insisting that you can't possibly fit one more thing into your morning! I'm asking your Inner Critic to trust me on this one and give it a try for seven days. Whatever your Inner Critic chatter is around this idea, know that it's all resistance to a new way of being. Stop and take a deep breath. If you aren't experiencing any resistance, that's terrific—don't go looking for any!

Making Yourself a Priority

One of the ways we let others know that we care about them is by making them a priority. Forgetting to make *yourself* a priority lands you in the *I don't matter* place, which is the gateway to the land of victimization. You do matter. You are important. Give yourself permission to be the priority at the beginning of your day. Try it. You'll likely discover that whatever happens the rest of the day, your Inner Coach can make a touchstone of whatever you did for yourself that morning and use it as a reminder that you cared enough about yourself to place your needs first for 15 minutes. This is an extremely effective and proactive daily practice for strengthening your Inner Coach.

Whatever the circumstances and events of the day, give to yourself first. Although it may seem backward to think about putting yourself first, keep in mind the safety demonstration you are given when you fly. The flight crew explains what to do if there's a drop in cabin pressure: if you're traveling with a child or someone who needs help, put on your own oxygen mask first. Think about it. If you put on the child's mask first and then pass out, you're no longer able to help yourself *or* the child. By putting on your own oxygen mask first, you're in a better position to assist others. Similarly, by caring for yourself first on a daily basis, you have a solid platform from which to more effectively support others.

Make the decision: first thing every morning for 10 or 15 minutes, your needs come first. Try it on this week, and watch what you attract into your life!

RE-PATTERNING STATEMENTS
FOR MAKING YOU A PRIORITY

I **forgive** myself for believing that everything else has to get done before there is time for me.

I give myself **permission** to do something first thing every day this week just for me.

I **choose** to stop leaving myself until last, by nurturing myself first every morning.

I'm **free** to nurture myself first this week.

When I nurture myself first, I **feel** as if I matter.

I **matter,** and I nurture myself first.

Have you heard yourself say, "When there is time, I'll . . ." and then discover that there just *never* is time. You're so busy doing things for your partner, the kids, your boss, your volunteer commitments, and your friends that you begin to wonder, *What about me? When will it be my time?* Taking care of everyone else first often means you don't address your own personal needs. It's most beneficial to develop the habit of attending to *your* needs first! When your foundation is solid, you can easily give to others without codependency and without the exhaustion that comes when you give and give and give without giving to yourself!

As a young woman, I would wait until everything was done before I did things for myself. With working, volunteering, managing our home, and spending quality time with my kids and partner, there was never time left for me. I pushed myself to a state of exhaustion and developed a chronic health challenge. I had two choices: put myself first or stay ill. Through the process of healing, I discovered that it wasn't selfish to give to myself first; it was necessary. I began the habit of doing so every day.

Leaving yourself until last lands you in the *victim* place. You would never consciously put yourself there, but that's what happens when you make decision after decision that everyone else's needs are more important than yours. The good news is that you're the one who landed yourself there, so you don't need to negotiate with anyone other than you to move over the line to *feeling good about yourself.*

Quick Reflection:

CHOOSE ACTIVITIES THAT NURTURE YOU

Choose a simple activity that you don't normally do that nurtures you. In your journal, create a proactive plan for the upcoming week. List seven nurturing things that you can do for yourself first thing, beginning tomorrow morning.

You can choose the same activity every day, or try a variety of different ways to nurture yourself and explore what works for you. Beside each one you've listed, write how you feel whenever you do that. Here's my example:

Going for an early-morning walk	⇒	peaceful
Doing yoga	⇒	invigorated
Looking at photos of my trip to Europe	⇒	adventuresome
Journaling	⇒	heard
Taking a bath instead of a shower	⇒	pampered
Watching the sky lighten with a cup of tea	⇒	content
Googling my dream vacation	⇒	excited

Use your plan for tomorrow morning as the activity (A) in this re-patterning series, and focus on the feeling that it will bring you.

RE-PATTERNING STATEMENTS FOR SELF-NURTURING ACTIVITIES

I **forgive** myself for believing that I don't have time to _____ (A).

I give myself **permission** to _____ (A) for 15 minutes first thing tomorrow.

I **choose** to nurture myself and feel _____ (⇑) by starting my day tomorrow with _____ (A).

I'm **free** to nurture myself and feel _____ (⇑) first thing every day this week. I matter!

Whenever I _____ (A), I always **feel** _____ (⇑)!

I **am** nurturing and _____ (⇑) to myself by _____ (A) tomorrow morning!

Use these Re-patterning Statements as you go to sleep to reinforce your decision to implement this new daily practice. Change it nightly with the specific nurturing activity you are doing the next morning to send a strong message that your subconscious mind will work with while you sleep.

Get Creative!

Marg was a client I met a decade ago. All the things she had dreamed about doing after she retired weren't happening. Her days were full, but there was little fulfillment. Her time was her own, but she never seemed to get to what she really wanted to do. A loving and thoughtful individual, Marg was always taking care of others first, and her own needs were never a priority. She was continuing the pattern she'd learned as a first-grade teacher. By evening she was just too tired to do anything for herself.

When I asked her what she really wanted to be doing, she confessed that she loved to paint. While she was working, she imagined exploring her creativity, but so far in retirement, her canvases remained empty, her brushes untouched. Her studio was fully set up and waiting, and every time she passed the door, unconsciously a part of her felt ignored and hurt, a victim to the activities of her day that kept her from her studio. I asked her how she would feel if she painted every day. Her face lit up and she responded, "Free and happy!"

We did some re-patterning around giving to herself first, and feeling deserving of happiness and freedom, and then I suggested that she begin her day with 15 minutes of painting, before anything else. I encouraged her to make what she loved a priority in her day, to give to herself first. She was resistant; there hadn't been time until now, so how could she possibly find a slot in her day to paint. Simple—she didn't need to find the time; she just needed to *create* it.

What if she painted the very first 10 or 15 minutes of her day?

What if she woke up, stretched, got out of bed, and after a quick bathroom stop, put on her painting smock right over her pajamas and went into her studio?

What if the first part of every day were reserved for her to feel free and happy with her brushes, paint, and canvases?

What would that be like? Would the rest of her day be different? Would she still accomplish everything else that was important?

Would she commit to the new daily practice for a week before she decided whether it would work?

Her answer was yes.

Marg agreed to paint every morning before she made coffee or got dressed. Before she did anything for anyone else, she agreed to give herself 15 uninterrupted minutes. When we touched base at the end of the week, she was thrilled. She no longer felt like a victim. Her days were productive and happy, and she felt free. She'd been in her studio painting every day, and the new daily practice was definitely becoming a habit.

She loved the new start to her days, and she was hooked! She extended her painting time and confessed to me that one day, a delivery arrived and she realized only after she had closed the door that she was still in her painting smock and pajamas at 2 P.M.! Within a year she had a show featuring her work. For the last ten years, she has enjoyed a part-time career of creating her own art and teaching others to tap into their own creativity through painting. Free and happy? Absolutely! And it all began with 15 minutes, devoted to her.

* * *

Giving to oneself first thing is a favorite exercise of my clients. They all report increased (⇑) feelings, and a calmer and more productive way of being throughout the day. By giving to yourself first, you send the message to your subconscious that you matter and you are worthy of nurturing. You are resetting your reticular activator. It's the quickest way out of the victim trap that I know. It doesn't really matter what you do during that first 15 minutes, as long as it's just for you. Be present with your feelings as you engage in this nurturing activity. You may wish to make a cup of tea and read, meditate, or write a note to a friend. You may choose any favorite activity, like playing an instrument, visioning, or singing. What really matters are the feelings you are consciously experiencing while you are doing your nurturing activity. Be clear with yourself: you're giving yourself the first moments of the day because you come first.

I know it doesn't sound that profound or earth shattering, but you've undoubtedly experienced the opposite situation on those mornings when you wake up 15 minutes late and your whole day craters around you. You feel as if you're running behind all morning. That late start can put you into panic mode, which follows you out the door and into your entire day, coloring all of your experiences. You may also have commiserated with a colleague who arrived late to an afternoon meeting saying, "What a day! I slept in and have been trying to catch up all day."

So what about creating the opposite scenario?

I strongly encourage you to really nurture yourself first thing in the morning for a week. Before you go to bed, decide how you will nurture yourself tomorrow morning. If it works, go to bed a bit earlier in hopes of waking up sooner, or set your alarm if you need to. Beginning your day by doing something *just for you* increases feelings of self-love and feeds your Inner Coach. Spill that into your whole day and observe how something this simple dramatically improves the quality of your life.

What Is Intention?

As you develop the daily habit of putting yourself first, you will notice how that sets the pattern for the remainder of the day. Whenever I miss my daily practice, I feel off all day. Out of sorts and not myself, I feel as if I am operating without direction. Engaging in the practice of nurturing yourself consciously first thing every day sets you up with a focus. This awareness is key. More than just clearing away old issues, Belief Re-patterning actually adjusts your reticular activator through conscious intention setting. The reason this practice is so powerful is that you're sending a clear message to your mind to focus on *you* as an important priority. Your RAS will then give your subconscious the instruction to continue focusing in that direction for the rest of the day.

When I began talking about this with my clients, I discovered that many of them hit the ground running and didn't stop until they collapsed exhausted into bed after a full day, feeling that there was even more to get done the next one. I saw how stressed they were. I also had clients who calmly progressed through the day, taking events in stride. These individuals had a true sense of fulfillment and seemed to sleep well. They also had something else in common: clear intention. Conscious intention *sets* your reticular activator, screening the information and experiences of your day. Without clear intention, your reticular activating system (RAS) is set to *react*. With clear intention you are proactively setting your RAS to *respond* to everything that is in the direction of your desires.

Knowing where you're going is always instrumental to arriving successfully, but in the midst of a big change, it can be challenging to know exactly what you want. During the tough times in my life, I knew that being very clear about my goals was important. I created vision boards and made lists of what I wanted in a partner, a home, and my career. I was heavily into the *go, go, go* of daily life. I was doing all the right things, yet manifesting anything seemed to take forever. Then I would become frustrated with myself and the whole process, which naturally created more frustration. The Law of Attraction works both ways. Positive thoughts and affirmations create positive things, and low-vibration thoughts and actions create low-vibration things. I wanted to manifest my reality from the right side of the line and create positive, high-vibration results.

I understood the importance of intention and taught the concept in my classroom but knew I was missing a piece. I felt as if I were *going through the motions*. The activities worked, and I knew they would work better with a clearly stated intention. The challenge I was facing at the time was that I couldn't seem to find mine. I absolutely knew the general direction I was headed, but the specifics eluded me.

In my early 30s, while I was struggling with that debilitating health challenge, my only goal was to *get well.* I had achieved that, despite the prognoses I was given over and over, so I knew I could manifest my dreams. I had focused on simply becoming well. I hadn't thought as far ahead as what I would do once I *was* well. Things had changed significantly for me, as they do when you overcome major challenges. My priorities had shifted.

It makes logical sense to know where you are headed before you begin. I understood that clear intention allowed my mind to work subconsciously in the direction of my dreams. It's like having a destination in mind when you set off on a trip. It doesn't mean that there won't be side trips or that partway along, you won't change your mind about where you want to go. I agreed with Yogi Berra's observation: "If you don't know where you are going, you will wind up somewhere else." For heaven's sake, for years I had been teaching my junior-high students that they needed to set intentions and create goals for themselves, and here I was, confused and stumbling around! Before the health challenges, I had been a high-achieving goal setter who could do this so easily, yet every time I would enter into a conversation around goals, my Inner Critic was there, putting me down for being unclear about my own intentions.

The Answer Was Right in Front of Me

One weekend I pulled out all my old scrapbooks, diaries, and journals looking for answers. After keeping them for years, I studied the outpouring of my desires, the working through of my frustrations, and the visualization of my dreams, and realized: I had been focusing on the activities of *do,* and on the material results of *have.*

As a teenager and young adult, I filled scrapbooks with pictures of cars, houses, and dream trips. As an adult I moved from scrapbooks to cardboard posters that I compiled annually and hung on my office walls. I looked at the poster boards in chronological order and realized that over time, there had been a noticeable shift. When I was experiencing health challenges, the pictures, understandably, were of healthy and happy people, good food, and nature. What kind of car I had or how my house looked was no longer important to me. This made sense because I no longer looked at my life in the same way. I couldn't articulate it, but I knew I had come to a new perspective of profound awareness.

The poster boards changed again once I regained my health. One poster had red hearts all over it, with a sprinkling of pictures and loads of cutout words. Another had images of candles, candles, and more candles, and was covered with words. There were very few pictures and lots of colorful words cut out of magazines; all of those words were feelings or ideas that created a strong emotional response when I read them. And then I got it! In that moment I realized I was no longer focused on the *do* and the *have.* I now cared about the *be.* My intentions were all over those poster boards in words like *calm, knowing, harmony,* and *freedom.*

I sat back in my chair and looked around my office. The walls were literally papered with quotes; inspirational poems; sayings; and single words of high vibration, like *love, believe,* and *trust.* The message was clear: I had surrounded myself with emotional words like *possibilities, hope,* and *courage* that encouraged my *be*-ing.

My intention was how I wanted to *feel.*

Now this may be completely obvious to you, but for me it was another pivotal moment. I realized that the *be* of anything was my intention. As my awareness grew and the disparate pieces began to form into a cohesive knowing, my attention was drawn to a scrap of a note I had stuck on the wall with a yellow pushpin:

"You are a human being, not a human *doing.*"

All of the signs were around me, and I began to see clearly.

Intention is all about *be.*

Goals are all about *do.*

The results are the *have.*

How I wanted to *be* surrounded me on my office walls. I knew my intention! In the middle of my office, surrounded by my diaries, journals, poster boards, and all the supportive words tacked onto the walls, I celebrated.

✳   ✳   ✳

Perhaps you've been focused on doing. If you have, you are not alone. Our whole society seems enamored with what we are doing and making certain that we keep busy. Clients come to me with challenges, wondering what they should *do*. I help them learn to define themselves by their states of being rather than their actions. Setting an intention by determining how you want to *be* in a situation is very different from wondering what you should *do*. What to *do* comes out of how you want to *feel*. When you begin with feeling the emotion, the actions and activities that create more of that feeling will naturally follow.

RE-PATTERNING STATEMENTS FOR BEING

I **forgive** myself for believing that it works to focus on the *do*.

I give myself **permission** to focus my attention on how I want to feel, the *be*.

I can focus on *do*, or I can focus on *be*; I can't focus on both at the same time, so I consciously **choose** to focus on the *be*.

I am **free** to set my intention in every situation by focusing on how I want to feel.

I feel most like me when I'm feeling _____ (⇑), _____ (⇑), and _____ (⇑).

I **am** consciously *being* by creating the feelings of who I really am.

Creating Calm

While I was celebrating my newfound realization, I stopped in my tracks. No wonder I had been having challenges with being focused and productive! Even though all the messages were supportive, the sheer number was mind-boggling. *Too much of a good thing,* I heard my Inner Critic say.

How did I want to *be?* I looked at my most recent poster board. Front and center, I had pasted: "Find calm and go there daily."

I set about creating calm in my office. I found a big purple photo album filled with plastic sleeves and got started. Piece by piece, I removed the scraps of paper from my walls, placing them into the photo album, and began what became my first *I Am* list. Some papers had several words of being: *content, fulfilled, happy, successful.* Some had one: *heard, valued,* or *loved.* All of the supportive *be* words from my walls I wrote on my *I Am* list. As I was doing so, I realized I was engaged in a running internal commentary. My Inner Critic and Inner Coach were agreeing and disagreeing.

When I wrote *patient,* my Inner Critic observed, *With others but not always with yourself.*

I wrote *compassionate, loving, and fun,* and my Inner Coach agreed, *Yes, you are!*

I wrote *abundant,* and my Inner Critic said, *Not yet.*

So I began a second list, one I titled "I Am Becoming."

Try This One Practice:

I AM AND I AM BECOMING

If you have vision boards and old journals, review them to see the ways you have been defining yourself. In your journal, create two lists, one titled "I Am" and the other "I Am Becoming." Look around you. There are indications everywhere of who you are and what you want to become. How you define yourself comes out in your words and actions, and others pick up on the energy that you are emitting. Making these two lists will help you observe the way that you currently are, reinforce the aspects you embrace, and point out the direction for growth and change.

You may not have all the answers staring you in the face as I did in my office 20 years ago, but you do know the qualities and emotions you want to feel. You may have thought of this before, or this may be new for you; either way both an *I Am* and an *I Am Becoming* list are helpful for creating your own Repatterning Statements. These lists will include emotions, feelings, and ways of being. Start with the attributes you've identified throughout the exercises and reflections you've been doing in your journal. These lists, like the oxygen masks that appear when the cabin pressure is compromised, will support you in challenging situations.

Whenever you don't know what to *do,* switch your thoughts to how you want to *be* and let the *do* come from that place. Create the feeling you want to experience, and trust that the results you desire will arise from it. Stating your intention gives your subconscious mind a conscious framework. Because the language of your body is emotion, use a *feeling* word. The Re-patterning Statements have a clear intention, with a focus on experiencing less of the (⇓) feeling and more of the (⇑) feeling. Allow these (⇑) states of being to *be* your reality. Your thoughts and actions come out of your emotions. Your results always reflect your feelings. Changing your thought patterns creates feelings that are in alignment with your desires, and then those goals, dreams, and desires are manifested.

How you start your day matters. How you feel makes a difference. "Begin with the end in mind." Living intentionally is consciously increasing the amount of time in which you are on the supportive side of the line. You give yourself permission, you choose, and you're free to be who you really are.

❋　❋　❋　❋　❋

Chapter Fifteen

IT'S YOUR JOURNEY:
Define Your Way of Being

✳   ✳   ✳

*"We all have our own roads to travel, and we all have our
own lights to shine. It's been a long, hard lesson, but I've
come to understand I was meant to be who I am."*

— STEVE SESKIN AND ALLEN SHAMBLIN

I believe that all we are ever asked to be is true to ourselves. When we try to be someone we aren't or live up to someone else's perception of how we should be, it feels uncomfortable. Steve Seskin and Allen Shamblin's song "To Be Who I Am" (**www.steveseskin.com**) really encapsulates what it's like to be living someone else's dream for you and have the courage to step into your own. What you think you have to do often comes from old beliefs based on what you think others expect of you. Those expectations may be real or simply your perception. Either way, this is your life, and you are the creator. It's not too late, and you haven't wrecked your chances. You are meant to be comfortable in your own skin. Life is a process of coming to know yourself.

When my girlfriend Dale and I were introduced, we both had that instant click. Call it recognition or total acceptance, but we felt like old friends who had just met. Although we live thousands of miles apart, we pick up where we left off, and our times together are nurturing and life giving for both of us. Dale once described her observation of the impact of re-patterning on me in this way: "The part of you I've always loved shines brighter each time I see you, and the part of you I'm not so keen on shows up less and less." This is what being who you really are does for you! Belief Re-patterning becomes a way of being in the world that brings you to the authenticity you seek.

Many people are spiritually homesick. Recognizing that they want a spiritual connection, they often go after it before connecting with themselves. When you engage inwardly and learn to be present with your inner conversations, what you seek appears. Where your mind, body, and soul align is the place of heart. Belief Re-patterning supports you in learning to live from this heart space, and enables you to show up as who you really are in all areas of your life.

Recently I was speaking with another longtime friend, who is four years away from retiring and was just appointed as vice president of a large company. As I congratulated her, she began telling me that she was so unhappy. Yes, she had the money and security, the prestige and the recognition, but her heart and soul were withering. She told me that she had come to the realization that she would never live her dream.

Trying to encourage her, I shared my perception when I had heard the news of her promotion: that she was going for it in her last couple of working years so that she would have the funds to enjoy her retirement. My perception discouraged her, and she said she wasn't sure she would make it until then. She told me she wasn't even sure how she ended up where she was; it had never been her intention. She got caught up in the *doing* and let go of the *being*.

No one but you knows what you truly want from your life, and you can change course anytime you choose. It really isn't about what you're doing, but rather the way of being that you bring to any and every situation. It truly is the relationship you have with yourself that counts.

This book is filled with effective ways of training your subconscious mind to automatically move to supportive thoughts, and I've left my simplest suggestion for last! It takes about a minute in the morning and will positively affect everything you do for the remainder of the day. Make a conscious habit of choosing one specific (⇑) feeling first thing in the morning and then framing your day around it. This simple act exercises both your conscious and subconscious minds, giving you something uplifting to focus on while you are doing other things. It creates new energy within you and causes a higher vibration to be emitted. This results in new outcomes and supports you in proactively creating, defining, and reinforcing the positive belief you choose for yourself.

Consciously Choosing a Feeling

At the beginning of each day, pick a word denoting an emotion or state of being that is energetically on the supportive side of the line. Consciously choosing an (⇑) emotion for your mind to focus on and your body to feel creates a subconscious *walking meditation* throughout your day. The word becomes both a guide and a touchstone, providing direction for everything you do.

This simple daily habit allows you to consciously build your perception of who you believe yourself to be by *trying on* new feelings. It integrates seamlessly into everything you do by giving your reticular activating system a clear intention. I've shared this easily incorporated and powerfully impacting daily practice with thousands of individuals. You'll find it an incredibly effective way of raising your energy and focusing your thoughts.

Every morning, you prepare yourself physically by showering, getting dressed, and brushing your teeth. Consider Belief Re-patterning to be your emotional hygiene. You'll feel more in flow by consciously choosing a (⇑) word each morning. Your first thought of the day sets the pattern: be proactive about choosing that pattern.

I suggest you start by selecting one word daily from among those on your *I Am Becoming* list you began in the Try This On! Practice in the previous chapter. You may also want to reinforce the (⇑) words from the Re-patterning Statements you've created in your journal. Any positive emotional word will do. I discovered that many of my clients found choosing one challenging, so I pulled together *Poster Full of Possibilities* and the booklet *Pocket Full of Possibilities: 999 Words to Up Your Vibration* to support them in creating this daily habit. Both of these publications, as well as a downloadable application for this daily practice, are available at **beliefrepatterning.com**.

Here is an excerpt from the 999-word list to get you started:

Abundant	Focused	Loving
Authentic	Gratitude	Nurturing
Blessed	Grounded	Peaceful
Calm	Harmony	Possibility
Celebrate	Honoring	Purposeful
Confident	Inspire	Rise above
Courage	Joyful	Trust
Create	Kind	Understood
Empowered	Lead	Value
Energized	Learn and grow	Wise

Try This One Practice:

CHOOSE YOUR DAILY WORD

Choose a different word of intention each day. Once you have identified it, write it down in your journal or on your calendar, or use a dry-erase marker to write it on your mirror or window. Use the word in a simple series of Re-patterning Statements:

RE-PATTERNING STATEMENTS
FOR DEFINING YOUR DAY

I **forgive** myself for believing that the way
things have been is the way they have to stay.

I give myself **permission** to focus on being
_____ (⇑) today.

I consciously **choose** to increase my feelings of
_____ (⇑) as I go about my day.

I'm **free** to explore new ways of being
_____ (⇑).

I've **felt** _____ (⇑) when I _____.

Today I experience **being** _____ (⇑).

In the morning, use the word to preview and plan
the tone of your day. Excellent times to do this are
while you're in the shower, making your breakfast, or
driving to work. Identify and clarify your intention
while you go about your morning routines to focus
on (⇑). If your word is *compassionate,* think about the
activities you have planned and set the intention to
be compassionate with yourself and others in these
specific situations. Your Inner Coach might preview
your day like this: *When I have the meeting with Joe at*

work today, I will be compassionate about his needs and mine. I will bring compassion to my conversation with my daughter. When I am driving around doing errands, I will be compassionate toward myself.

Go about your day, and should challenges present themselves or you find yourself at a decision point, employ your Inner Coach to focus on your word of intention: *What would be the most compassionate choice for me?* or *What would a compassionate person do in this situation?*

Observe your (⇑) word in others you encounter during the day or while you are watching television: *Camille is being very compassionate with Natalie* or *Mark handled that situation in a compassionate way.*

If it isn't already there, you may wish to add the word to either your *I Am* or *I Am Becoming* list.

In the evening, just before going to sleep, review your day using the intention word; for example, *Today I experienced compassion when I met with Joe. It worked well. I'm so happy I was compassionate with that gal at the store; things work better when I remember that. And being compassionate with myself made all those errands easier! While I was watching the news, I was thinking how the world would work better if we were all more compassionate with ourselves and each other, just as Dave was when he asked how he could help, and . . .*

This lets your mind work with the (⇑) feelings all night, and it's a good practice for calming you for sleep.

Focusing on your word of the day and keeping a list of the positive attributes you've re-patterned also provides great leveraging ability. Since beliefs always group together, you can tie a new (⇑) attribute to an already existing (⇑) belief. Put these words in places where your subconscious will notice them. Putting your words on your screen saver or on a sticky note beside your mouse is a great idea for anyone who spends time at a desk. Individual words carry their own unique energy. When I renovated my office, I put (⇑) words behind the wood paneling, under the carpet, and on the underside of the planks of the steps leading to my office door. After reading Masaru Emoto's book *Messages from Water* (HADO Kyoikusha, 2002), I put the words *love* and *abundance* on the water pitcher I use with clients! I've also been known to write my words on a piece of paper and place it under my pillow or on the bottom of my chair.

I receive more feedback from this exercise than any other. A student of personal development, Betty-Ann was excited to add the two-day Belief Re-patterning Basics course to her tool kit. Partway through the weekend, she mentioned having had difficulty breathing ever since a traumatic experience several years prior. We did a ten-minute re-patterning session specifically around her breathing. She was surprised by the immediate change in her ability to breathe more deeply. A few days later I received this delightful e-mail from Betty-Ann: "Did you know how incredibly easy this work is? Upon waking Monday morning, the only thought in my awareness was my breath. What an exceptional feeling of connectedness and belonging! My word for Monday was *healing,* and for Tuesday, it was *free.* I am in awe of this work!"

You know there is potential within you. You can feel it, and you are on a journey to realize all the possibilities available to you. To illuminate this journey, you need to shine your own light within you. Developing the sub-conscious habit of supportive inner conversations, in combination with consciously choosing how you want to feel in any given situation or circumstance, allows the *You* that is *you* to shine. You live from a heart space, with your body, mind, and soul in alignment. Decisions in all areas of your life are made from the side of the line that creates (⇑) feelings in your body. This is your new normal.

Everyone wants to know how long *it* takes, as if there were a *done* button that pops up. Every bit of re-patterning changes your inner conversations and creates lasting and wonderful results. You've learned skills that support a more positive belief in yourself, and the world around you reflects that.

The thing I've discovered about learning is that the more I know, the more I uncover what is yet to be known. The same applies to Belief Re-patterning. It takes a very short time to re-pattern one belief, and the changes that occur are tangible. How long *it* takes depends on what "it" you are looking for.

A gal I didn't recognize ran over to me at the shopping mall to thank me for the 10 minutes I had spent re-patterning with her during a 60-minute seminar eight years ago. She excitedly introduced me to her sister and her mother, saying, "This is Suze. She's the woman who changed my life!"

I'm grateful that Belief Re-patterning was able to provide that support, and I replied, "Thank you, but it's *you* who changed your life. I simply helped you find the keys to unlock the door; you are the one who walked through it!" Those few minutes resulted in a profound change for her.

How long will it take for you? You've noticed changes as you've explored Belief Re-patterning. Clients often ask me, "When will I be done?" as if they have some kind of bucket filled with issues and blocks that needs to be emptied before they can get on with *real* life. When you focus on dealing with issues and fixing what's wrong, you end up with more issues to deal with and more problems to fix. When you focus on being (⇑) and creating supportive beliefs, significant and lasting positive change is the natural outcome. Those of us who have embraced this way of living, by implementing a conscious daily practice of re-patterning, experience a life of purpose filled with love, joy, and inner peace.

Trusting Yourself

You're building trust in yourself, and your Inner Coach is stronger. Consciously re-patterning for a few minutes every day will increase your subconscious mind's ability to *flip the switch to positive thoughts*. You understand more about how your thoughts affect your energy and how your energy transmits out into the world. You know you respond to whatever happens, and you know how to proactively strengthen yourself so that your reactions are in alignment with who you really are and what you truly want. You are creating your personal reality through loving and nurturing inner conversations. You have a dream, and living your truth guides your steps on your path. You have let go of wondering what to do, and know that the focus is on how you choose to be. Re-patterning your beliefs allows you to move purposefully in the direction of your dreams. Believing in yourself and coming to know who you really are means that you live from your heart, in genuine alignment.

Belief Re-patterning brings to your awareness the learning processes you have been using for your entire life. You didn't arrive with an owner's manual, but throughout this book you've created one just for you! I trust that re-patterning will be a welcome and supportive addition to the tool kit you're developing to create a way of being that is true to you.

Holding a Space

Have you ever watched a child learn to walk? We encourage and cheer them on at each stage. At no point do we judge them by saying, "You're just a little kid; you'll never walk. Look at how you fall down every time you try; why don't you just give up?" We don't give them ultimatums like, "If you don't learn to walk by next Tuesday, that's it; find another place to live." We'd never put conditions on the outcome by saying, "You must walk just like me," nor would we place expectations on their learning with a comment like, "If you don't walk 20 miles a day, what's the point?"

We know that their learning is happening in perfect timing. We celebrate each small gain in their ability—learning to stand, to pull themselves up, to walk around the coffee table—until all of a sudden, they are running quickly, and we are trying to catch up! They go from crawling to running nearly overnight. As supportive adults, we hold a space for children while they are learning. By holding a space, I mean that even if they can't do it now, we believe they can and will be able to at some point in the future. We encourage them in the direction of their dreams by believing in their ability.

Hold a space for yourself. You are learning, and just because you haven't done something before now does not mean you can't from now on. Holding a space for yourself to learn and grow in the direction of your dreams encourages your Inner Coach.

Truly holding a space from the *right side* of the line means letting go of ultimatums, judgment, expectations, and conditions. Here's a practical and basic analogy. Your oven holds a space for the cooking of a wonderful meal. It doesn't tell you what ingredients to use or how to put them together. It doesn't insist on a timeline or get frustrated with you when you don't use it every day. The oven simply holds a space for you to put into it whatever you decide, for however long, as frequently as you desire. It's ready and waiting for your direction, and it holds the space to transform into dinner the ingredients you've gathered, the recipe you've chosen, and your preparations. Hold that kind of a space for yourself to transform your desires into reality.

When you're learning anything new, focusing on strengths works, and learning to love yourself is no different. At times love for yourself may be buried under regret and pain, but you do love yourself. How do I know that? Your actions reflect your beliefs. You are holding this book. If you didn't love yourself, you wouldn't have picked it up. Since you already love yourself at some level, you have the capacity to deepen that love in more meaningful ways. Increasing your capacity to love and honor who you are and encouraging all of your positive attributes to shine will bring about the changes you desire.

Where this empowered way of being will take you no one, not even you, can know! When you learned your letters and numbers, your teacher had no way of knowing how you would take those skills and apply them in your life. Your teacher just knew that it was important for you to have them. Through Belief Re-patterning you've learned the skills of *flipping the switch to positive thoughts*. Who knows where this will lead you! I excitedly anticipate hearing from you about what is manifesting in your life.

I have shared with you the impact and effect that Belief Re-patterning has had on my life, and the lives of many, many others. Now it's your turn. What do you notice? How has your interaction with this book supported you? My blog and contact information can be found at **www.suzecasey.com**. I'd love to hear your experiences as you integrate Belief Re-patterning into your way of being.

Thank you for taking this journey with me, and for making the decision to grow and step into this way of being. I'm not a fairy godmother, and I don't have a magic wand, but if I could give you three gifts, they would be: the ability to truly believe in yourself, the courage to show up as you truly are, and the confidence to act from that place of authenticity.

✳ ✳ ✳ ✳ ✳

NEXT STEPS

* * *

"My willingness to change my thinking is changing my life."
— LOUISE L. HAY

Welcome to your lifetime of new experiences! With every breath, every day, everyone has the opportunity to change the way things have always been. In each and every moment, you design your world. Re-patterning will change it in ways you can only imagine. Your life experiences will shift. Feel your way into who you truly are and consciously live from a supportive place of joy and compassion. How will you know where to begin? You already have. *Feel into* your being. If something feels good, strengthen and reinforce it with Re-patterning Statements. If something feels bad or uncomfortable, you know you can and will re-pattern it.

By using the Re-patterning Statements in your day-to-day activities, you'll find calmness in your way of being in the world. Approach life from the right side of the line, and be gentle and loving with yourself while doing this work. It is all perfect! You are doing exactly what you need to do to learn, grow, and move in your chosen direction in every moment and with every breath.

I encourage you to be empathetic with yourself. You will get to the other side of whatever challenges arise. Hold on to that faith and show compassion for yourself. Your *now* is always changing, and your inner conversations are shaping your future. It's not too late. New breaths are being taken every day, and the opportunity to change the way things have always been is ever present. Take a new breath, *feel into* who you truly are, and consciously create your life.

Clients frequently ask me how often they should re-pattern. Re-patterning Statements are a conversation you have *with* yourself rather than words you recite *to* yourself. The more you consciously practice the technique, the faster you will develop the habits that create positive thinking. The scripted statements throughout the book are samples to help you learn to build your own supportive inner conversations. The exercises are great daily practices. Pick what feels right for you.

So many people wait until they are physically ill or in emotional pain before taking care of themselves. Thank yourself for being proactive and integrating re-patterning exercises into your day-to-day experiences. I often compare Belief Re-patterning to keeping your house. Every day, you make meals, do dishes, and wipe counters. You regularly vacuum your carpets, do laundry, and make your bed. You tidy up as you go along. The exercises in this book are like these daily and weekly housekeeping activities. When it comes to cleaning out closets, organizing your garage, or tackling the stuff in the basement, it's always good to have help, and working with a practitioner will shorten the time frame for real and effective change. Similarly, if you're planning on renovating or building an addition to your home, you have the skills to re-pattern on your own, but renovations are more successful and are completed faster when you call in a professional. There is a community of Belief Re-patterning practitioners available to support you, whether you're working through some old patterns that have held you back, or are embarking on a new venture.

Curious about how you can extend your learning beyond this book? I would be honored to guide you further in your personal and professional development. I've taught thousands of individuals to re-pattern; their results are positive, measurable, and profound. I welcome your comments and questions on my blog. In addition to my Hay House Radio program, I offer individual coaching programs and Belief Re-patterning courses that will deepen your abilities, and I invite you to extend your learning through "Flip Your Switch from Inner Critic to Inner Coach," the five-hour introductory course that reinforces and extends what you've learned in this book. I am always open to an invitation to offer this course in your community or workplace, or you can join in online. You'll find details on all of my course offerings at the Belief Re-patterning website: **beliefrepatterning.com**.

Mastery of Belief Re-patterning is a bit like mastering the game of chess. You can understand all the moves and rules, but there is an art and an intuition that comes from playing the game. With consistent practice, you'll become confident in your ability to use Belief Re-patterning. Integrating the technique into your life will support you to live in a new way.

Everyone experiences the same number of hours in a day. Every moment, we each choose how to live our lives. Commit to raising the vibration of your inner conversations, improving your interactions with others, and creating more positive and life-giving days.

Your thoughts *do* affect your world. Your world *can* affect your thoughts. You are the determining factor!

Forgive yourself for believing that change is difficult.

Give yourself **permission** to change your experiences with ease.

Choose to speak to yourself the way you would speak to a friend.

Experience the **freedom** of being who you really are.

Affirm yourself with acknowledgment and gratitude.

Surrender to the truth of *you.*

I am committed to supporting others who choose to live well. Join me in creating the reality of a world where all individuals show up as who they really are, valued and respected for their uniqueness. It begins by valuing and respecting yourself through developing the habits that will automatically flip your switch to positive thoughts. Each of us is on a journey of creating the *best "me"* possible. Travel well—I look forward to our paths reconnecting!

"Man often becomes what he believes himself to be. If I keep on saying to myself that I cannot do a certain thing, it is possible that I may end by really becoming incapable of doing it. On the contrary, if I have the belief that I can do it, I shall surely acquire the capacity to do it, even if I may not have it at the beginning."

— ATTRIBUTED TO MAHATMA GANDHI

Acknowledgments

* * *

Thank you, Louise Hay, for creating a home for this work. Your vision and clarity has changed the world. I couldn't have begun to imagine your contribution to my life when I first picked up *You Can Heal Your Life* more than 20 years ago. Your very presence is an inspiration; your work is a beacon.

My gratitude goes to Reid Tracy and Cheryl Richardson for the mentoring you provided at the Movers and Shakers event in Toronto in September 2010; your workshop provided exactly what I needed to bring this work to a wider audience. Thank you for balancing straightforward reality with heart and passion. I also appreciate the clarifying coaching with fellow attendee Scott Loring.

To the members of my readers' panels: The book is stronger because you each shared your unique insights. I am truly grateful to each of you for your encouragement, and I am humbled by your commitment.

Bev Gersbach, your enthusiasm and perspective provided the support I needed for the revisions! Brenda Holden, as both book retailer and practitioner, your point of view was valuable, and you brought joy and light to my writing. Carrie Broadstock, my practitioner on call, you supported my personal re-patterning when the writing presented challenges. Charis Birchall, your willingness to seek clarity and ask for what you needed continued to amaze and stretch me. Dave Casey, I value our transition from partnership to friendship. Your thoughtful reflections provided richness to my writing. Eileen McGann, you believed in this work from the beginning. Your clarity of observation kept my writing focused. Jackie Bell, your fresh perspective and great questions helped me hone my thoughts. Mark Maitman, your astute comments, incredible writing skills, and superb editing brought me back on track more than once. Thank you for being willing to delve into a topic that wasn't on your radar. Myrt Butler, you boosted me whenever I wandered next door. Tracie McTaggart, your one last look before we went to print reassured my Inner Coach! Val Denn, thank you for the writing haven of your fish shack in Nova Scotia and for the incredible organic nourishment of body, mind, and soul.

I am so appreciative of my office team. Flo Simpson, I bless the star that brought you into my life. You managed my practice so that I could focus on writing. I am also grateful for the creativity and clarity Lisa Stangel brought, which went well beyond her amazing formatting and proofing skills!

Hay House editor Alex Freemon is a lifeline. Thanks for the clarifying chats, your steady way of being, your laser focus, and comments that always came from the right side of the line! The book is stronger because of you. And thanks to Nelda Street for your excellent work on the copyediting. My deepest gratitude and awe to the artistic abilities of Jenny Richards, who so wonderfully translated the manuscript into a book, and to Tricia Breidenthal for creating a cover that so beautifully captures the essence of Belief Re-patterning!

Thank you to the practitioners and apprentices, whose passion for this work inspires others! I value your dedication to bringing the best of you to the world. Specific thanks to Rita Lucas; your belief in the early days sustained me. Thank you for insisting that I teach you how to do this work! I am truly grateful to Trae Ashlie-Garen for the phenomenal support you provided as I clarified the Belief Re-patterning curriculum. Marnie Johnston, your consistent generosity of spirit is inspirational. Thank you for your compassionate and clear leadership.

In addition, this work would never have evolved to this place without the trust and willingness of all of my students and clients. Watching you step into your personal power confirms my decision to follow my own passion. Know that every time I hear from you, I am inspired to continue.

I am blessed to have amazing friends who held the space for me during the development of Belief Re-patterning. In particular I am deeply grateful for the trusted support of the two people to whom this book is dedicated. Thank you, Dale; you encourage me every time I stretch my wings. Our insightful conversations always bring me back to me. Your wisdom and grace coached me through the entire process. And to Kathleen, you've always held the vision. You ask great questions, give tough feedback, listen better than anyone I've ever known, and made certain I kept true to myself. Thanks for asking what it would take to write and publish the book. Your loving but insistent nudge in the direction of Hay House's Movers and Shakers event changed my life and the lives of many. Thank you.

I'm grateful to Ian for the creation of my work space: the perfect balance of an anchoring quiet haven and an inspirational vista.

To my cousin Allison, your belief makes a difference. Thank you for your loving heart.

Mom and Dad, I am grateful to both of you for encouraging and supporting my dreams.

Camille, Charis, and Dave, I am a better teacher and a better person because of you. I feel honored to be a parent of choice!

To the little ones who have shared so much so unconditionally by just being, you remind me to be present to the moment every moment. Grandbabies Casey, Jacob, and Natalie and my niece, Lyla, your hugs and smiles sustain me. Your perspectives on the world inspire me. How blessed I am to witness the development of your belief systems and learn from you. I love you more than I ever knew was possible.

And finally, thank you to *you* for opening up to the truth of who you really are.

Namaste.

About the Author

✳   ✳   ✳

While searching for answers to the health challenges she experienced as a young adult, **Suze Casey** drew on her knowledge of the learning process, which she gained from earning a master's degree in education and from her work as a classroom teacher, to support her in reclaiming her own physical and emotional health. This experience ultimately led to the development of Belief Re-patterning and her commitment to helping others overcome their challenges and live their lives purposefully.

After a 20-year career as a public-school educator and university instructor, Suze began building her thriving Belief Re-patterning practice in Calgary, Alberta, Canada. Since 2001, she has supported others to learn, grow, and embrace their potential through consultations, coaching, keynotes, courses, and corporate seminars. She continues to train licensed practitioners to meet the demand for this amazing personal- and professional-development technique.

As an author, Suze has created the booklets *PathWays: A Guide for Belief Re-patterning* and *Pocket Full of Possibilities: 999 Words to Up Your Vibration,* tools for supporting individuals in the re-patterning process. In addition, in 2011 she released the book *HealthKeeper: The One Place for Everything Regarding your Health,* further supporting individual empowerment by providing an easy-to-use guide for tracking your most precious asset.

Suze delights in working collaboratively with her clients to build the positive belief structures that will support them in creating what they truly deserve and desire. A dynamic, informative, and engaging professional educator, Suze has always been fascinated with the mysteries of the human mind, how we learn, change, and come to know our own truths.

beliefrepatterning.com
www.suzecasey.com
info@beliefrepatterning.com
1-855-286-9380 (toll free)

✳ ✳ ✳ ✳ ✳

HAY HOUSE TITLES OF RELATED INTEREST

YOU CAN HEAL YOUR LIFE, the movie,
starring Louise L. Hay & Friends
(available as a 1-DVD program and an expanded 2-DVD set)
Watch the trailer at: **www.LouiseHayMovie.com**

THE SHIFT, the movie,
starring Dr. Wayne W. Dyer
(available as a 1-DVD program and an expanded 2-DVD set)
Watch the trailer at: **www.DyerMovie.com**

* * *

ENOUGH ALREADY:
The Power of Radical Contentment, by Alan Cohen

FRIED: Why You Burn Out and How to Revive,
by Joan Borysenko, Ph.D.

JUICY JOY: 7 Simple Steps to Your Glorious,
Gutsy Self, by Lisa McCourt

TAPPING INTO ULTIMATE SUCCESS: How to
Overcome Any Obstacle and Skyrocket Your Results,
by Jack Canfield & Pamela Bruner

YOUR DESTINY SWITCH: Master Your Key Emotions,
and Attract the Life of Your Dreams!
by Peggy McColl

All of the above are available at your local bookstore,
or may be ordered by contacting Hay House (see next page).

We hope you enjoyed this Hay House Insights book. If you'd like to receive our online catalog featuring additional information on Hay House books and products, or if you'd like to find out more about the Hay Foundation, please contact:

INSIGHTS

Hay House, Inc., P.O. Box 5100, Carlsbad, CA 92018-5100
(760) 431-7695 or (800) 654-5126
(760) 431-6948 (fax) or (800) 650-5115 (fax)
www.hayhouse.com® • www.hayfoundation.org

✷   ✷   ✷

Published and distributed in Australia by: Hay House Australia Pty. Ltd., 18/36 Ralph St., Alexandria NSW 2015 • *Phone:* 612-9669-4299 *Fax:* 612-9669-4144 • www.hayhouse.com.au

Published and distributed in the United Kingdom by: Hay House UK, Ltd., 292B Kensal Rd., London W10 5BE • *Phone:* 44-20-8962-1230 • *Fax:* 44-20-8962-1239 • www.hayhouse.co.uk

Published and distributed in the Republic of South Africa by: Hay House SA (Pty), Ltd., P.O. Box 990, Witkoppen 2068 • *Phone/Fax:* 27-11-467-8904 • www.hayhouse.co.za

Published in India by: Hay House Publishers India, Muskaan Complex, Plot No. 3, B-2, Vasant Kunj, New Delhi 110 070 • *Phone:* 91-11-4176-1620 • *Fax:* 91-11-4176-1630 • www.hayhouse.co.in

Distributed in Canada by: Raincoast, 9050 Shaughnessy St., Vancouver, B.C. V6P 6E5 • *Phone:* (604) 323-7100 *Fax:* (604) 323-2600 • www.raincoast.com

✷   ✷   ✷

Take Your Soul on a Vacation

Visit **www.HealYourLife.com®** to regroup, recharge, and reconnect with your own magnificence. Featuring blogs, mind-body-spirit news, and life-changing wisdom from Louise Hay and friends. Visit **www.HealYourLife.com** today!

CPSIA information can be obtained at www.ICGtesting.com
Printed in the USA
LVOW061451240512

283130LV00001B/1/P